RUPERT BROOKE

THE MAN AND POET

by

Robert Brainard Pearsall

RODOPI N.V.

AMSTERDAM 1974

ISBN: 90–6203–437–3

For:
Christopher G.S. Pearsall
with love

TABLE OF CONTENTS

PREFACE

The lives and works of most minor poets — say Rochester, Bowles, and Whittier — can be encountered with cheerful objectivity by most critics. Other poets seem to engage critical emotions, and even critical passions. Rupert Brooke is an aggravated example of the second group. In earlier years he enjoyed, or did not enjoy, the love of dozens of people who knew him. Later, millions of strangers joined themselves to him sentimentally. Through a necessary reaction, he was sometimes hated even in life, and has been hated and scorned by quite a few people since. Both emotions, love and hate, have been intensified by his positions vis-a-vis the class-oriented educational and social arrangements of his milieu, by differences of life style, and by national politics. One does not get very far into biographies like those of Hassall (1964) and Hastings (1967) before realizing that praise and blame are being meted out to the poet's environments as much as to the poet or the poetry. Brooke is there, but, as it were, dimmed by Brooke's surroundings.

In this book I have tried to review Brooke's life and work against the background of society and politics, as must after all be done, but with a detached attitude and an analytic technique sufficient to separate the two concerns. Following Henry James and Winston Churchill, the modern biographers Hassall and Hastings (who agree on little else) agree that in Brooke's case a flat separation of "man" and "poet" would be arbitrary and misleading. I have nevertheless made the attempt. My program has not been to write two separate accounts, but to run the two accounts side by side. Though short and to him confused, Brooke's life had a kind of harmonious curve in which poetic activity and other kinds of activity worked with a neat reciprocity. Sometimes I find bridges across, and readers will often find more.

The increasing distance between Brooke's elite experience of school and university and the experience of the transatlantic general reader has caused me to describe Brooke's Rugby and Cambridge with some particularity. There are some discoveries still to be published about Brooke's personal life, but I have relied on

8

the manuscript sources, particularly the collection at King's College, more especially as they concern themselves with the development of his literary character. As an old soldier myself, I enjoyed presenting his short soldierly career. My critical evaluations rely on concepts of traditional structure, prosody, and imagery which he worked at and understood, and on simple psychological doctrines which he was beginning to understand when he died.

I owe thanks everywhere. Among printed books to which any writer on Rupert Brooke is heavily indebted are the *Bibliography* (1954 and 1964) and the *Letters* (1968), both prepared by Sir Geoffrey Keynes, and the rich *Biography* by Christopher Hassall (1964). In my work with manuscript and copyright materials I have enjoyed the generosity of the King's College Library, Cambridge, and the Rupert Brooke Trustees, and am very grateful. To Dr. A. N. L. Munby, who is both Librarian of King's and a Brooke Trustee, I have special obligation. Thanks for various kinds of hospitality to the British Museum Library, libraries of the Universities of Munich and Rome, the Henry E. Huntington Library, the Humanities Research Center of the University of Texas, and libraries of the University of California in Berkeley and Los Angeles. To Miss Annekäte Abels, Miss Evelyn Kuhle, Dr. Reinhold Schiffer, and Professor Ulrich Suerbaum, all of the Ruhr-Universität, Bochum, thanks for kindness and help of several kinds. Warm thanks to Arlene Epp, Trier-Kaiserslautern Universität. For important friendship and help, thanks to Mary Ellen Boyling and good sisters at the College of Notre Dame, Belmont, California.

Robert Brainard Pearsall

San Francisco

Chapter One

BEGINNING AT RUGBY

During the reign of Queen Elizabeth I, a Warwickshire grocer named Laurence Sheriff rose into affluence and court favor, accumulated money and prestige, and looked about for a way to share his good fortune with his fellow men. Though born in the village of Brownsover, he had built a house in the more important town of Rugby, and it was the boys of Rugby that he chose as first beneficiaries. Combining the income from his properties in Brownsover, Rugby, and London, he formed a corporative endowment under the laws of England, and set a school to going. As a boy in the neigboring town of Stratford, William Shakespeare may have contemplated the new establishment with interest. It enjoyed good management and favorable laws, and within a single century had brought itself to the attention of the leading families of England, the two universities, and the nation as a whole. In a country of institutions, it had become a significant institution.

By the end of the seventeenth century, Rugby School had formed a loose connection with its boarding interests, and occupied a cluster of new and old buildings near the center of the growing town. In the 1740's, when it had become a boarding-school serving the whole nation, it was moved to an open and spacious new ground off to the south. Here it swiftly developed residence houses, chapels, playing-fields, and libraries. The center of the curriculum was of course Classics, but around this center all the customary modern courses established themselves — modern languages, modern history, the fine arts, mathematics and the sciences. A toughly competitive spirit governed almost every activity, from Greek and Hebrew grammar to poetry-writing and organized games. It was understood that the men who were to be prelates and soldiers, parliamentary orators, and masters of exotic nations in Africa and Asia, would establish their strength and resilience of character through Rugby syntax, Rugby friendships, and Rugby football.

The town grew as the school did, though not always in harmony with the school. The small local industry slowly gave place to factories serving markets throughout the world. Methodist chapels, government schools, and cheap working-men's suburbs spread out from the center. Four railway lines made juncture at Rugby, and the city could boast the longest railroad platform in Europe. With urban development came urban problems. In addition to his school, Laurence Sheriff had built a little almshouse system, which seemed enough for the destitute of Rugby in 1567. Another had been added in 1707, but by the middle of the nineteenth century there were sufficient destitute to justify three much grander houses supported at the expense of government. The town and school maintained contact in politics, education, and social affairs. Rupert Brooke, for example, could join in Liberal and then in Socialist politics in his own city, and his mother could exercise her managing ways as political and social-work campaigner and in the important rôle of Justice of the Peace. But such connections were casual and fleeting, for by the years of the Brookes, Rugby School was part of Britain, and not part of any town.[1]

Writing his own idealized epitaph at the end of 1914, Brooke flatly declared for the nation as against any particular landscape or any particular society. Britain, England, the complexities of race and region, the stirring and beloved history, the skillful blending of traditions, the interest in opposites and contradictories, the luxuriant poetry, the relaxed handling of ideas and principles, the instinct not only for play but for fair play, and the sturdily humorous language which was enriching all the languages of the world — he declared himself a part of all this, coding it, as British poets do, with an allusion to the green landscape:

> A dust which England bore, shaped, made aware,
> > Gave, once, her flowers to love, her ways to roam,
> A body of England's breathing English air,
> > Washed by the rivers, blest by suns of home.

What is meant is not landscape, for landscape is a chancy and

---

1. See for example, A. Burgess, *Warwickshire* (London, 1950), and J. Burman, *Old Warwickshire Houses and Families* (Birmingham, 1934).

irregular matter even in Britain. What is meant, as Brooke goes on to say, is "the thoughts by England given." As a national and traditional institution, the school looked away from its temporary city of Rugby, and off over its own grassy slopes and fruitful orchards into the pleasures of green country and green thoughts. When a Rugby boy went fishing, he would fish in the Avon of Shakespeare and have somewhere in the back of his mind the fishing-philosophy of Isaac Walton. If the river had become dirty, it's was a temporary dirtiness, and could be remedied in time.

Time is always an element of thinking in Britain. Operating within their different areas of time, the traditional school and the new industrial town lived cheerfully side by side, if not together. The city developed, with its industries, a new city park and a handsome brick City Hall. The school rebuilt its chapel, added an indoor pool and a library building, and continued to concentrate landscape, history, tradition, competitive habits, and the rudiments of education, through the medium of tough young boys.

II

Like the founder of Rugby, the various founders of Rupert Brooke's family had emerged from obscurity in the period of the Tudor kings. The most successful of these emergent characters was Matthew Parker, chaplain to Queen Anne Boleyn in the reign of Henry VII, and a founder and head of the Church of England in that of Elizabeth I, but others also attained to national distinction. If there is a family pattern, it is the pattern of medieval characters turning gradually from the land to business, and from business to the learned professions, particularly education and the church. By the middle of the nineteenth century most of the grangers and businessmen had passed into history, and the members of the family were attending public-schools and universities, and entering the two favored professions, almost as a matter of course. The favorite University was Cambridge, and by Brooke's time the favorite college at Cambridge was King's. The Brookes were already part of the history of that college. There had been a traditional exchange of honors between King's College and the school at Eton; but, though educated at the lesser school of Haileybury, the poet's father had broken through the tradition by becoming the first non-Etonian to be elected Fellow of King's. In this way he "had made college history."[2] And when Brooke elected to attend Cambridge, and King's, he found another Brooke, an uncle, installed as Dean.

William Parker Brooke, father of the poet, had begun his teaching career with an excellent appointment as classics master at Fettes, a new but solidly established public-school near Edinburgh. Among his Fettes colleagues was Charles Cotterill, another career schoolmaster. Ruth Mary Cotterill, the sister of Charles, joined the school as a "lady-matron" or housemother. There was a courtship, an engagement, and undoubtedly a preliminary struggle for leadership in the new household. The marriage rites were conducted in the Cathedral of Edinburgh by Mary Ruth's own uncle, Henry Cotterill, who had recently risen to be Bishop of Edinburgh. Soon afterward, through the efforts of other friends and connections, William Parker Brooke was called back to England, to be Classics Master and Form Master at Rugby school. This was a career step of the highest importance. It instantly established the newly married Brooke, and all his family, in a position of honor in the British school establishment, and a position from which it would be possible to rise with some ease either in schools or in the Church. And even if he did not rise – as he did not – he was in the most honorable and most remunerative of all the classroom posts in Britain.

As a wife, Mary Ruth quickly turned manager. Photographs show Mrs. Brooke as a smart and pretty woman, slender and quick-looking under her fashionable late-Victorian clothing, with sharp eyes, a drilled certainty of posture, and an alert, inquisitive tilt of the head. Christopher Hassall, the main biographer of Brooke, describes her as "rather stiff," with "a certain toughness whose basis was a singular strength of character." She was neither a resting nor a restful type of woman. Hassall ventures to say that she "would make an ideal wife for a schoolmaster, providing the social front which he lacked." Her husband, Hassall adds, "could go safely on with his routine of Latin and Greek, while she managed the business of life." A less friendly voice might suggest that her toughness, strength, and business skills were too energeti-

2. Christopher Hassall, *Rupert Brooke, a Biography* (London, 1964), p. 19.

cally applied in the small circle of her family. At first these qualities were usefully engaged. With them, she manoeuvred her husband and herself into mastership of the boarding unit called Field House. The residential houses at Rugby were at that time run on a hotel basis, so that by careful adjustment of the costs, the housemaster, or in this case mistress, could operate the dormitory with a substantial profit. There was never any question about who operated Field House during the Brooke regime. In addition to being continually in control, Mrs. Brooke was continually inquisitive. It was her habit to probe and question every kind of happening. "She must known the why and the what and the how of all the boys under her roof." She was no open tyrant, of course, "and not unsympathetic, so long as you were doing exactly as you were told."[3]

For several years, before the movement to Field House, Mary Ruth and her husband adjusted to another in a small house at the edge of the school properties. Their first son, Richard, was born in 1881, and the third son, Albert, in 1891. Like his brothers, the middle son, the poet Rupert, was named for a most Royal and Royalist personage, an emphasis which Mrs. Brooke tempered politically by adding the middle name of Chawner, in a balancing tribute to an ancestor who, as a Puritan M.P., had helped to chop off the royal head. As a boy, Rupert often used all three names, or else the first and last with an initial, American fashion. It may be of significance that Rupert Chawner Brooke was born after the death of another child, a girl, in early infancy, and had stood, as a male, in contradiction to Mrs. Brooke's hope for a girl-baby to replace the lost one. In any case, the mother let her son cultivate the belief that he was not what she had wanted. Brooke apparently made an internal drama out of this matter, and produced a minor rhapsody about it in a later year when he drifted toward self-inquiry and self-torment.[4] The full force of his mother's personality did not fall on him in those earlier years. His older brother stood between; and so, very miserably, did William Parker Brooke.

There is hardly any question of the inadequacy of Brooke

3. Hassall, *Brooke*, p. 21ff.

4. *The Letters of Rupert Brooke*, ed. Geoffrey Keynes (London, 1968), pp. 338-39.

Senior, considered as a husband and father. Within a few years of his marriage Mr. Brooke had developed a sad, put-upon expression, with a troubled, indecisive mouth only half concealed by drooping mustachios, and eyes which popped anxiously towards cameras, as though he expected trouble and grief even from the passive lens. He became absent-minded, and was called "Tooler" by the boys on account of forgetfulness about buttoning his trousers-fly. His position vis-a-vis Mrs. Brooke was notorious. It was said that after dark she would send him forth to gather horse-droppings for the benefit of her flower-garden, and he was known to stumble away from domestic disagreements muttering, "It *is* so, all the same."[5] He became a poor teacher, wilful, crusty, and inefficient, and made no serious pretension of keeping up with developments in scholarship or the arts. Every man aspires to more than this. The means of his carrying-off were the arterial stiffening and strokes which come to frustrated men with "nerves." His eldest son Richard was recently dead — of dissipation and vague diseases, far from home, likewise ultimately the victim of "nerves." Rupert was in college by that time. He came home and experimented at living with his mother, and certainly by no coincidence became at that time the prey of "nerves," and the achiever of those health-bringing periods of relaxation then called nervous breakdowns.

III

As each of her boys grew into his teens, Mrs. Brooke entered him as a student of Rugby. The advantage of a Rugby preparation in education, contacts, and career opportunities, was of course tremendous. At the same time, residence at Rugby, and especially in the House controlled by their parents, presented some obvious hazards. The youthful Brookes were never "away from home" or "out of school" as other boys were; and their capacities for loyalty and tact were strained by their simultaneous identification with the administrative powers and the student powers. In response to the unusual family and school pressures, Brooke soon learned the trick of temporary illnesses and consignments to bed, and later, as the family grew in prosperity, of visits to watering-places and spas for rest and recovery. He was to

5. Hassall, *Brooke*, p. 38.

exploit this possibility in many otherwise unjustified trips to the English coast and the Continent.

These illnesses must be understood as a system, not as physical weakness. With them, Brooke combined a pragmatic endeavour to succeed in all possible activities of school life. The endeavour was supported by an alert and responsive intelligence, quick physical reactions, a well-knit physique, and that elaborate compound of winsome traits which is summed up as magnetic personality. The steadiness and solidity of his character shows up nicely in his early diaries:

> We ought to have had a letter from Dick [the elder brother] today but we didn't. He must have been out to sea and not able to post one.
>
> I did not finish my Euclid and have got to write out from memory *20* and *21*. I've got a cold and am not allowed to go to drawing.
>
> I did a vile Latin E.
>
> We were beaten today . . . . It was partly my fault.
>
> We easily won, the pitch was awful it was slanting with the wind right across it. We went in first and were out for 78, I made 8. Then they went in and made 21 so we won.[6]

The simplicity of these private communications was not maintained in Brooke's public life at Rugby. In this public life he early employed self-observation and self-criticism, and became both a realist and a showman.

Contrasted to his diaries, his letters are postured and role-taking almost from the beginning. Some of the postures suggest only boredom and weariness, and a love of words. For example, in a letter of age 13 he reports having lost ground both in the "sports finals" and in examinations, "wherefore my temper was exceedingly warm." These failures have cost him a scholarship award which his parents have wanted him to win —

> Wherefore an irritability of marvellous size possessed me and still possesses me . . . . Forgive my letter being strange in manner. The reason is that much trouble hath unhinged my brain; wherein I resemble Hamlet. And if you gaze closely on my portrait which I have sent you, you will see a wild look in my eyes, denoting insanity.[7]

6. Brooke Papers, King's College, Cambridge.
7. Brooke, *Letters,* p. 4.

"This grew" as Browning says. Another example came to Geoffrey Keynes from Rapallo, where Brooke had gone to recuperate from an unimportant illness:

> You express a polite (and probably entirely fictitious) desire to hear what I am doing and undergoing. I don't know why. It probably won't interest you in the least. However, it *can't* interest you less than it interests me so I will weary you by the account of what I do this afternoon, as an example. You can build the other 59 days of my visit from this. I hope you find it very exciting. (it is now 6 p.m.) [A careful, dull schedule follows.] And so on. About 9 I retire to bed with the cheerful prospect of another happy, happy day when I wake. Half the night perhaps I lie awake thinking . . . all the time I am profoundly bored. At intervals they drag me up to Genoa and round a picture gallery; which is wasted on me. I say "How Beautiful! " at every fourth picture, and yawn.[8]

Brooke's ready pen manufactured hundred of pages of this kind of empty reportage. Gradually the stiffness went out of it, and the posturing toned itself up to more delicate species of irony and innuendo, with highlights of true observation.

> I am filled with a cruel desire to torture you [he wrote, again to Keynes] by describing at length the expedition we made yesterday to Fiesole. How we had tea on the hillside and squabbled about Browning and others. How the sun began to set across the plain beyond Florence; and the world was very quiet; and we stopped taling and watched: and how the Arno in the distance was a writhing dragon of molten gold, and the sky the most wistful of pale greens.[9]

Contrived though they are, such letters represent a serious and honest search for a prose style.

Brooke concluded his Rugby career as Head Boy, and developed a wide but not universal popularity among his fellow-students. He was amused by the romantic crush a boy of another house developed for him, but himself developed no crushes of any kind. Later he was to be regarded as a brilliant mediator between people, and a solver of people's problems; but at Rugby few people came to him with intimacies, and he did not offer inti-macies to others. He relied upon objective achievements for general approval, and meanwhile saved his friendship for a few

8. Brooke, *Letters,* p. 15.
9. Brooke, *Letters,* p. 17.

boys, and one or two girls, whom he regarded as benevolently disposed toward him, and as being safe. Whether schoolmates or outsiders, his friends had to be exactly of his own generation. He patronized people younger than himself, and dreaded anyone who was significantly older. The bulk of his correspondence is therefore addressed to a bare handful of friends — for the most part quiet, listening kinds of people like Geoffrey Keynes and Duncan Grant, or, a few years later, Edward Marsh and Maurice Browne. Even to such people he cannot be said to have habitually opened his heart. He was never a shy boy, but he was always wary.

IV

Throughout his four years as a Rugby student, Brooke tried to maintain a balanced life. He competed eagerly in sports, and rose to play both football and cricket for the School. Boxing pleased him and he became one of the good boxers at his weight. His mother had become interested in Liberal Party politics, and he devoted hundreds of hours to campaigning for now-forgotten candidates, and against such government positions as the ungraduated income tax and the South African war. Like most boys in the school, he spent some time in service of schools and camps established for the welfare of poor boys from the city slums. He got to London often, and liked to attend plays, musicals, and pantomines during his visits. George Bernard Shaw was the great playwright of those years, and Shaw's coolness of manner and irony of statement undoubtedly contributed to Brooke's own later habits. The Rugby scene provided an armed and uniformed militia company, the Rugby Rifles. Brooke drilled and shot his way upward through the ranks of this unit, and achieved the position of Cadet Commander. Some group photographs of the unit taken in 1906 show his easy dominance of the uniformed boys, as well as his frank interest in the camera lens. There is a certain simplicity in the military processes, at least in theory; and Brooke undoubtedly enjoyed this simplicity as a counter to the entanglements of his ordinary life.

A person who writes usually begins his efforts very early. Some rhyming efforts of Brooke date from as early an age as seven. At ten, after playing with Virginia Woolf (then Virginia Stephen) at the sea shore, he commenced a magazine of his own.

Its only issue contained an essay on some sights he had seen as a traveller, a short story about two slapstick burglars, and the beginning of a fantasy called "The Final War: A Tale of the War for the World in 1899." Brooke was not yet a Rugby student, but the format of this manuscript magazine is based on that of the *Meteor*, the regular Rugby magazine. A few years later he was writing stories, essays, and a good deal of poetry, and was a regular contributor to the *Meteor* itself. When the *Meteor* sagged under faculty censorship, he contributed to its underground supplements, the *Phoenix* and the *Vulture*. He showed determination as well as skill. Rebounding from his failure to win the school prize for a formal poem in the winter of 1903-1904, he competed again, and won, in 1905-1906. At the same time, he was sharpening his tools by regularly competing in a national poetry competition run by the *Westminster Gazette*. Sometimes he won, more often not; but this steady system of writing under competetive circumstances was undoubtedly of technical advantage to him. All told, he published 25 items in the *Westminster Gazette* and its sister organ, the *Sunday Westminster*.

Brooke was companionable as a writer, and many of his works and themes are connected to particular acquaintances. Did Virginia Woolf invoke his muse when they played together in the sands as little children? It was after that experience that he first broke into prose fiction. Among his earliest male friends, friends going back indeed to a period before Rugby, was James Strachey, the younger brother of Lytton Strachey. Brooke and the two Stracheys evaluated each other in an amusing triangular system of letters dated 1906. A lucky circumstance made him the classmate of Geoffrey Keynes, who long afterwards was to prepare his Bibliography and edit his letters.

> It does not often happy [Keynes wrote] that a poet has a recording angel at hand in the shape of a bibliographer from the very beginning of his literary career.... Though I was not, at so early an age, a conscious bibliographer, my admiration stimulated my natural instincts in that direction, and I immediately became a sort of press-cutting agency for Brooke's work.[10]

10. Geoffrey Keynes, *A Bibliography of the Works of Rupert Brooke* (London, third edition, revised, 1964), pp. 14-15.

William Denis Browne, whose name was shortened to Denis, was another early intimate. Browne's real love was for music rather than poetry, but by asking for lyrics to his compositions he stimulated Brooke's interest in this direction. This friendship held until Brooke's death, which Browne witnessed. Browne had scarcely buried his friend when he was killed in his turn, at Gallipoli.

There were also two slightly older literary friends, both residents or part-residents of Rugby. One was Arthur Eckersley, who had written fiction and plays, and was a regular contributor to *Punch*. The other was St. John Lucas. Lucas had entered the legal profession after Oxford, but generally lived in Rugby and preferred literature to the law. An able translator and editor, he was to prepare the standard Oxford University Press anthologies of both French poetry and Italian poetry. More important, he wrote both poetry and novels of his own. A thoroughgoing Oxford aesthete, in the line of Oscar Wilde and Ernest Dowson, Lucas was faithful to the programs of the Decadent movement of the 1890's. His idea of the pure in art featured lost lilies, pale visionary sins, silk and lacquer and white-skinned boys and girls, lovely priests driven mad by their passion for ruined ladies, exotic diseases, unnamable deaths, and the other *bibelots* of the movement. From him Brooke learned to respect both the arrogant vaunts of Wilde and the silvery images of Dowson. The decadent manner soon invaded Brooke's letters, and he amused himself and his friends by attitudinizing in it. The wit of Wilde became —

> There are two classes of Rugby schoolmasters: those who insult Beauty by ignoring it, and those who insult Beauty by praising it.
>
> How hateful are the feet of the middle-aged.
>
> Venice is an American colony, chiefly peopled by Germans.

— While the damp sweetness of Dowson became —

> An opium flavored cigarette circled wreathes of odorous pallid smoke.
>
> The evening will be ... purple with the dying sunset and odorous with young spring.
>
> I sat in the vaporous gloom of St. Marks in Venice and, gazing on the mosaics, mused of all my religions, till ... the grand altar changed to an altar of Moloch, the figure of Mary grew like Isis, and the fair Byzantine Christ was lost in the troubled form of Antonius.[11]

11. Brooke, *Letters,* passim 1903 through 1905.

Unlike Lucas, Brooke did not take this manner very seriously. His decadence often slipped into satire, as when he created what he regarded as the top possible metaphor, proposing that the moon was "like an enormous yellow scab on the livid flesh of some leper." When he was serious, indeed, he disowned the manner, as when, in Venice, he said "I was really miserable, being modern and decadent in an ancient eternal city."

The friendship with Eckersley and Lucas was of great benefit to Brooke. Besides its provision of serious practical criticism, it illustrated the possibilities of literature by presenting to Brooke two examples of actual writers whom it was possible to take seriously and yet to handle with familiarity. Their correspondence contained a good deal of pretentiousness and empty image-dropping, and a great deal of mere silliness. But in submitting his ideas, his sayings, and his actual poems to the criticism of these friends, Brooke was taking the sober first step towards a life in literature. In a quiz game he entered at this time, he certified that his "ambition" was "to be at the top of the tree in everything," and his "idea of misery" to be in "ignorance, poverty, OBSCURITY."[12] He was never in danger of ignorance or poverty, and as the years ran along he began to judge that the question of "OBSCURITY" could be best settled by embarking on a career in letters.

12. Brooke Papers, King's College.

Chapter Two

RUGBY POET

The Temple Library, named for a headmaster of Rugby who had gone on to become Archbishop of Canterbury, was luxurious, quiet, well-maintained, and seductively filled with old books and new books. Brooke became a regular reader in his first year at Rugby. He read history, biography, politics, and the standard British prose-writers, and paid especial attention to the newer poets and some of the older ones. His diaries and notebooks show him making a few literary starts in prose; and he actually published both stories and essays in school magazines. But his emulative interest was in the English poets.

According to Lord Dalton, who was Brooke's close friend at Rugby before beginning his career as a Labor politician, Brooke's early favorites were Swinburne, Meredith, Belloc, Arthur Symons, Ernest Henley, J. M. Synge, and W. B. Yeats.[1] One quickly adds Oscar Wilde, Walter Pater, and Henry James, among the prose writers. These were all contemporaries or near-contemporaries, and Brooke found them interesting for their often disturbing subjects and vaguely revolutionary theories, as well as for their technical skill and energy. Though officially neutral towards the Romantics (all but Keats) and officially at war with the great Victorians, he had Tennyson's rhythms and phrasing in his head, and admired very many poetical developments in the work of Browning. At Rugby he was not very interested in the great line of Tudor and Stuart dramatists, or in the drama as a literary discipline. Like every countryman of Shakespeare, he nevertheless contemplated the possibilities of the dramatic form. The main result during the Rugby years was an effort which might have been called *Pierrot.* Not much remains of it beyond the Dramatis Personnae, which lists, after "Pierrot," "the Lady," "the harp player," "Pan," "the King," and, rather oddly, "Christ." The play

1. "Lord Dalton's Memoir of Rupert Brooke" and other Mss., King's College Library.

must have been like Dowson's then-famous Decadent play called *The Pierrot of the Minute* (1897). But Brooke did not advertise this effort even in personal letters, and we know little about his intentions with it.

The attraction of Browning is of considerable interest, since Browning was one of the solidest citizens of that Victorian republic of letters which Brooke's generation longed to overthrow. But it was Browning's verse that first awakened Brooke, then aged nine, to the possibilities of straight talk in verse. Later, in college and after, his opinion seems to have changed. He assured one friend, Erica Cotterell, that Browning was "not a very good poet" (and added "Blake is"), but advised his lover Katherine Cox to read Browning all she could. His letters and papers contain several parodies of Browning's most familiar poems. His more definitive considered view was developed in 1912, in an essay commemorating the centenary of Browning's birth. In this essay he spoke of Browning's many-sidedness as a man, amazing versatility as a poet, and deep-rooted membership in the British middle classes "whom the nineteenth century made, and who made the nineteenth century." He laid the overwhelming popularity of Browning to the proposition that Browning had brought poetry nearer to the lives of his readers. "Morris, Tennyson, and Swinburne sang of Greek gods, paganism, youth and beauty, things remote from Victorian England," Brooke asserted. "Browning's interest was in Christianity, passion, and the amazing heart of man — matters that some part of England knew." One could have Browning or other Victorians, but not both.

Closely connected to Brooke's own development, as he left the attitudes and slogans of the Nineties behind him, was his concern with the immediacy and familiarity of Browning's best verse. "Browning's ideas were new, for poetry," he wrote; "and they came in a flood." Browning's ability to catch the mood of a moment or a single person led to "harmonies" often new and "chords" often harsh. His most significant triumph, Brooke argues, was in his double feat of bringing common language and common personalities into poetry. British novelists as well as British poets had learned from him "the vivid and intimate analyzing of various types of the human heart . . . the true psychological life." And all subsequent writers had owed to Browning "the liberation and making real of English poetry" through

Browning's reform of the poetic language. "It is due to Browning's influence that emotions of poetry can be expressed by words and forms and phrases of everyday life," he urged. "Such constructions as *they've* or *they're* or *isn't* are allowed to modern poets again, as they were to Shakespeare and his contemporaries. *They've* may seem an insignificant and ludicrous monument. But it is not."[2]

Later Brooke transferred the development of spontaneity, immediacy, and vernacular phrasing from Browning to Donne, as was proper since Browning himself had worked under the influence of the earlier poet. Among the other seventeenth-century poets, Marvell was most useful to Brooke. Since part of his creed was a total rejection of the Eighteenth Century, he never discovered the vernacular delights of Pope's *Dunciad* and "Epistle to Arbuthnot," or the colloquially vibrant work of small poets like Prior and Robert Ferguson. He was too fond of ideas and too concerned with independent creation to be a trustworthy critic of older literature. Still the views he took were critically respectable, and as he developed away from his half-serious concern with the Decadent movement, he was able to work a good selection of these views into his own program. Meanwhile, as a clever and versatile but not brilliant student-writer at Rugby, his work ran out along two separate lines. One of these we may call "official" verse, since it takes the main road of the reflection-plus-resolution poetry upon which British lyric poets have depended from the beginning. The other is the Decadent verse which, for Brooke as for the nation, offered an interesting and slightly shocking temporary detour.

II

After his tenth year, Brooke uttered the official kind of poetry as naturally as a tree utters leaves. His early letters are full of verse of all kinds, much of it directed in critical ways toward the discipline itself. He wrote parodies of Browning, Housman,

2. *Internationale Monatsschrift für Wissenschaft, Kunst und Technik*, Feb. 1913. Ms. in Brooke Papers, King's College. An English version (from the Ms.) is in Christopher Hassall, ed. *The Prose of Rupert Brooke* (London, 1956), pp. 102-107.

and Swinburne, as well as amusing "occasional" poems such as his quite competent sonnet "To My Lady Influenza." And he wrote serious poems on love and death.

To maintain the balance which was the key to his popularity at Rugby, Brooke was careful not to seem to take his more serious efforts seriously. His references to his own poems are almost always mocking or ironic; and when he allows some seriousness to break in, as in a few of the letters to Eckersley and St. John Lucas, he always expresses doubt or rejection. At the same time, his letters how how hard he drilled himself at the basic poetic techniques. In several notebooks he is seen working out quite serious problems in prosody. Two notebooks show him assembling line-schemes and rhyme-schemes for rigidly disciplined forms such as the tercel, rondel, villanelle, and viralay. He had an early interest in the conflicting theories of the sonnet, and maintained this interest until his death. He jotted down lines which seemed to have special possibilities because of their sound or imagery — for example, "And all the people have gone into their houses," which follows a classic rather than English pattern. He loved words and liked to jot down lists of words which seemed worth remembering. One such list gives "scotomy," "glibbery," "inexpugnable," "inennerable," and "dizzling," with a score of similar cameos. However, he early learned the trick of simple style, and learned to value clarity over all.

Working in this way, steadily though not single-mindedly, Brooke developed a considerable technical skill even as a schoolboy. Perhaps without wanting to, he picked up and utilized many of the standard themes and manners of nineteenth-century British poetry. Like many boys who are undergoing a serious educational experience, he leaned especially toward the profound, and fell into the tones of earlier boys, his betters, who had gotten away with the profound most successfully. In "The Path of Dreams," written at sixteen, he is very like the youthful Tennyson:

> Strange blossoms faint upon the odored air,
> Vision, and wistful Memory; and there
> Love, twofold with the purple bloom of Triumph
> And the wan leaf of despair.

In "The Return," taking a stance suggested by Shelley, he longs for "old fires on the old grey altars" and "old gods [in] their shadowy haunted grove." In "Afterwards" he imagines himself a person who —

> ... nurses in his festered soul a slave's dull hate
> For this interminable Hell of life; and yet
> Shrinketh from ending it, in fear of what may wait
> Behind the pitiless Silence of Eternity.

Here he falls below most of his possible models. Sentimentality, the bad tendency to express emotions excessive to the cause, is the hallmark of this and a dozen poems surviving from the Rugby period. Most of these were never preserved or collected by Brooke, and remain as examples of his desiring "to write" rather than to write some particular thing.

Always a competitive person, Brooke sought for competitive situations in which he could practise against rivals. One opportunity arose through a weekly writing-contest supported by the *Westminster Gazette*. In this department of the widely-circulated journal, a fresh literary problem was set every month by the conductress, Nancy Royde Smith. As each month's competition closed the best entries were printed, and a substantial cash prize was sent to the winner. Brooke became a regular contributor while still at Rugby. He submitted work under false names like "Sandro" and "Teragram," and won his share of awards and honorable mentions against the nationwide competition. Often the problems were simple enough. "Write a Sicilian octave, descriptive not reflective," was one; and though Brooke was not the winner that time, his octave was printed in the journal. But sometimes the problems were of extreme complexity. Christopher Hassall reprints one which in its manifold and complex instructions demanded that sense be made of rhapsodic nonsense, and afterwards reduced to the narrow room of a sonnet. Borrowing his tactics from sonnets of Wordsworth and Rossetti, and squeezing the long specified catalog of things, events, emotions, and people, into fourteen quite elegant lines, Brooke easily won the first prize. When the first set of competitions was reprinted as *The Westminster Problems Book,* six of his contributions were included. He told his mother with satisfaction that his principal competitors were the professional writers Rose Macaulay and Lord Curzon — "a pleasant fact."[3]

3. Printed with other juvenilia in *Poetical Works,* ed. Geoffrey Keynes

Brooke demonstrated the same keen competitiveness in his drive to win the annual Prize Poem award at Rugby. The rules of the 1906 effort specified rhyming verse with "The Pyramids" as subject. Brooke's response ran to 108 lines loosely but faithfully rhymed, and carefully varied in length:

> How many nations have they seen arise
> And widen into greatness, and at length,
> Though fair and firmly set to all men's eyes,
> Yet sapped from within
> By luxury or sin
> Fall swiftly from the glory of their strength
> Humbled in far-spread ruin with the lies
> That subtly wrought their downfall.

He described the fall of the prestige nations, first Egypt, then Babylon, China, Greece, Rome and Napoleon's France, not failing to assert that his own Britain, which was the prestige nation in 1906, faced the same decline "out of all history, vanished quite away." Brooke's competently stylized poem won a special mention, but was not the winner. Brooke's letters show that he was nettled. He charged at the next year's competition with his own special combination of energy and irony, keeping the problem before him as he traveled on the continent and rested on the English seashore. The subject was "The Bastille," and rhymes were again acceptable. This time, Brooke's entry ran to 141 lines, and his rhymes were less faithful but also less obvious. The message was again of an acceptable profundity. He described the Bastille in all its centuries of evil, and then in the bright and bloody hopefulness that accompanied its fall. But then —

> How the bright glory of that early faith
> Is faded now, and tarnished; for we know
> Not by one sudden blow
> Are peace and freedom gained; nay even yet
> Grey poverty, and Sin that poisoneth
> Eat out men's hearts, and tyrranous wealth is strong,
> And almost we forget
> Because the night of suffering is long.

(London, 1946). Unless otherwise specified, quotations from Brooke's poetry follow this edition.

The poem concludes with some lines on the human race as it moves on, "bitter with gloom and sorrow . . . Blind in the utter night," toward the gleam of a "star of an infinite tremendous hope." The hope is for an "Eternal Day" — that is, a Christian eternity, something that would be acceptable to the judges of the contest, but which Brooke never believed in. The parts of the poem which Brooke really meant are the parts in which capitalism and plutocracy are challenged, for by his last year in Rugby Brooke was a Socialist. This time his poem won the prize.

Brooke read his poem to Rugby and the friends of Rugby on Speech Day, and was suitably sarcastic about the occasion in his letters.[4] His poem was officially printed by the School, and printed again by his pleased mother. For his prize, he won the works of Browning and the works of Rossetti. There was a definite intelligence behind the selection, but Brooke made fun of that too.

III

In 1907 Geoffrey Keynes grew tired of Brooke's '*fin de siècle* brand of Byronic melancholy," and asked his friend to give it up. Brooke responded with more *fin de siècle*, saying that his author friend Arthur Eckersley was "tremendously excited" about Keynes, and judged him to have "the most decadent face he had ever seen." But he added, more seriously, that the "pose" of "pessimistic insincerity" suited his own needs. Still more seriously, he opened the general question of imitation as opposed to reality, and realistically described his life as mostly imitation. He spent his time, he reported,

> pretending to admire what I think is humorous or impressive in me to admire . . . Even more than yourself I attempt to be "all things to all men"; rather "cultured" among the cultured, faintly athletic among athletes, a little blasphemous among the blasphemers, slightly insincere to myself. . . . There are advantages to being a hypocrite, aren't there? [5]

One who describes oneself as a hypocrite has uttered a paradox by which he can be judged as the opposite, and Brooke knew this very well. But Keynes's protest and his own response undoubtedly

4. Brooke, *Letters*, p. 145.
5. Brooke, *Letters*, p. 73.

mark a change in Brooke's personal style, and shortly afterward in his poetic style. It was time for such a change. The images and mannerisms of Decadence were beginning to make his correspondence unsound, and were no longer adequate to express the subjects of his verse.

These images and mannerisms had, however, served a useful purpose in focussing the confused intentions of his boyhood. There exists an unpublished manuscript of a prose tale in two parts, written when Brooke was most under the influence of St. John Lucas and marking the high point of Brooke's serious interest in Decadent themes. The story features a beautiful young priest as hero. The priest lives among a typically decadent temple-population, including "white acolytes," gong-players, stunned and feeble worshippers, and "all the beggars and diseased who swarmed like maggots." To tempt the priest into damnation, a woman enters the tale. She is fantastically beautiful, of course, and "her virginity flashed like a sword; and her terrible purity whispered intolerably passionate suggestions." Seeing her, the priest "flung his arms wildly out to the radiant mystery, his lips stammering unconsciously shameful words." It is in this story of diseased environment and unforgivable sins that Brooke develops his most prized decadent simile, making the moon "like an enormous yellow scab on the livid flesh of some leper." Under this nauseous moon the priest shrieks: "She is more beautiful than Mary and more gentle than Christ. In the shadows of her hair my soul flutters like an entangled moth."[6] And there is lots more of this.

The verse of this period, most of which also stayed in manuscript through Brooke's life, is full of sonorous and classically off-the-meter verse expressing the same second-hand Decadence:

> Looking only at your lip's scarlet
> And your hot violet eyes;
> Drinking the wine of Hell, the gall of Heaven,
> From your body's chalice: till the even
> Called to me with desolate cries.

As in the more traditional juvenile poems and poem-parts,

6. Brooke Papers, King's College.

these efforts stand as a reminder that Brooke still had nothing much to say. They show also, however, that he was continuing with his technical studies and exercises. It was undoubtedly exciting for him to rhyme "wanderer" with "sea-water" and "quiet mysteries" with "far plaint of viols is", and to image forth "God's own hand" to emplace "as aureole / My song, a flame of scarlet, on your brows." His greatest mechanical triumph was probably the line, "Or the soft moan of any lute-player", which concluded "Ante Aram," a poem he liked and printed twice in his own lifetime.

His almost continual reference to death and permanent loss is of interest not because of its originality but because of its ubiquity. The death note of Decadent writing caught thousands of hearts at the turn of the century, and still catches many a youthful heart. But it seldom sticks as it stuck to Brooke. He had already sounded the note in the earliest poem printed by his editors, the "God Give" of 1903:

> Ah yet, if it could be
> That as the long day drew to evening
> And the light
> Drooped like a weary lily o'er the sea
> Sudden across my sorrowing
> Healing and fragrant, with the fragrant night
> Thou should'st come back to me,
> And I should see thy delicate feet returning,
> The tremulous eyelids of my old delight,
> And all the beauty and supple youth of thee.

One notices that not only death and loss but also youth and beauty are celebrated, though with great limpness and passivity. In a stronger poem, "The Lost Lilies," written two years later, Brooke moves the same way:

> Ah, surely here at length oblivion
> Shall crown my wandering, and this dim perfume
> Cover away remembrance of things gone
> > In scented groves and passionate warm gloom.
> > Surely more sweet the rose's gentle kiss
> > Than the pale sorrows of my lost lilies.

7. Hassall, *Brooke,* pp. 130-32.

Even in in this poem, Brooke's suspicion of Decadent limpness is growing clear. He gently removes himself from the situation with cool observations such as "Thus in my youthful bitterness I spake" and "Joy for a time seemed but Satiety," two observations which might have served as slogans for the whole movement. But the two linked themes of youth and death were never to depart from his verse.

Within a few years he had finished with the Decadence as a system of poetry. He returned to its manners occasionally, and found its collection of overstressing adjectives such as *unspeakable, tremendous, passionate,* and *infinite,* hard to leave off entirely. But he eschewed the un-English rhythms, and made fun of the experimental phonology:

> I love a *scrabbly* epithet
> The sort you can't ever forget,
> That blooms, a lonely violet
> In the eleventh line of a sonnet.

In a fine critical poem written at Cambridge after he had discovered the "serene utterance" of the Elizabethans and Jacobeans, he deliberately attacked his schoolboy models as "the clamorous, timorous whisperings of today." In his attack, called "A Letter to a Live Poet," he announced himself "sick" —

> Of simple-seeming rhymes, bizarre emotions
> Decked in the simple verses of the day,
> Infinite meaning in a little gloom,
> Irregular thoughts in stanzas regular,
> Modern despair in antique meters, myths
> Incomprehensible at evening,
> And symbols that mean nothing in the dawn.

IV

Like many sons of schoolmasters, Brooke early developed a taste for laying down the law. In the letters he wrote at Rugby he took strong positions on writers, among other things, and usually won arguments when there were differences. However, these letters were written swiftly and the opinions given in them do not represent reasoned criticism or thoughtful preference. Though the letters are always interesting, they tell us less about the development of Brooke's critical talents than do a series of critical papers which he prepared for reading before the Eranus Society, a literary group which – according to Brooke – was lumpishly unliterary, and much in need of his instruction. His efforts included papers on Hillaire Belloc, on the nineteenth-century James Thompson, on Swinburne's *Atalanta in Calydon,* and on "Modern Poetry," where he ran rather erratically across the field as it stood in 1905.

Of the paper on Belloc, some sentences on style are of interest. Belloc's style, as young Brooke thought, was "free, limber, and bubbling with a pleasant pride." His prose was "properly self-conscious indeed and wilful, but not too artificial." Like a good garment, his style draped "to reveal, not to conceal, his figure." This resumé accurately describes the style for which Brooke was working, and runs significantly opposite to the Decadent style. The paper on *Atalanta in Calydon* was "full of beautiful quotations," as Brooke reported in a letter, but the quotations were not all. His scholarly remarks fall into two main groups, one on Swinburne's remarkable style and one on issues in the theory of tragedy, where Brooke "advanced the most wild and heterodox and antinomian theories, and was very properly squashed." That the Chorus in *Atalanta* climaxed its observations with "a tremendous indictment of the Unknown, the supreme evil, God," was important to Brooke's thinking, for he was already working towards a transcendental or cosmic view of literary tragedy. His paper on James Thompson, author of *The City of Dreadful Night,* was carefully thought out, and written up in an aphoristic but not quite pedantic style. Part of the argument in favor of Thompson was merely *ad hominum.* The drunken and despondent Victorian had lived a terrible life, Brooke said, and had deserved a better one. But the rest of the paper quite adequately set forth the solid qualities of Thompson's work – his bitter pessimism, his massive despair, his tender sympathies, and above all his unflinching honesty as a poet. "He had the courage of his convictions, a phenomenon rare enough in England," wrote Brooke. "His work naturally enough does not appeal to a large audience: he is not often pretty or weak; among all his temptations and vices, he never committed the sin of writing down to the common taste."

Brooke's reading of his paper on Modern Poetry was his last public act at Rugby, and a number of the masters, including his father, crowded in to hear it. Considerable sections of this paper have been printed, and it has been thought important as a contemporary review of the poetry of England in 1906. It is a well-planned paper, beginning with a learnedly humorous exordium on the Muses of Greece and Britain, and concluding, in the plan at least, with a tactically balancing peroration on the modern spirit as expressed by modern poets. Actually the paper spilled over its design and became a series of comments on the six or eight recognisable schools or movements of that time, and on the six or eight poets Brooke especially admired. Among the schools, he naturally had the most to say about the Decadents, his praise of them resting mostly on the proposition that they had developed naturally and necessarily as Decadents because of their position in a diseased cultural and intellectual setting. Working within decay and death, they produced more of each. Exhausted like their environment, they turned from greatness to littleness and glory to disease.

> When you have listened to the great poets and their gospels, and grown weary of the hot splendour of their passion, the high majesty of their genius, or when, with some other moderns, you have explored the abysses of your own soul and return sick and frightened, it is pleasant to find refuge in such poetry as this, that strives not for the eternal verities, but deals in faint exquisite words of a man's vision, being full of "a pathos too young and too frail ever to grow old."

In a cancelled passage, Brooke added that the "true decadence," by which he meant true perversion, came when "the dweller in cities . . . puts on a smock over his frock-coat and goes out into the country, hoe in hand, singing unnaturally simple harvest-songs." This assertion would have constituted a slash at both the Celtic Revival poets, headed by Yeats, and the Edwardian poets who were just then taking the defined form of a movement. Brooke probably cancelled it because of the cheaply verbal way he had shifted the semantics of the word Decadent. Anyway he was in a hurry. He went on to praise A. E. Housman, W. E. Henley, and Rudyard Kipling on various grounds, clearly noting that they spoke of both Death and Empire. He made the association clear by specifying that the "political poetry" of William Watson was "national rather than imperial," and that Irish poets were what they were because they belonged to "a weak nation" which could not "accept the imperial spirit." Brooke himself was not an imperialist, but such ideas were capable of being readjusted in the eight years that remained before 1914.

The catholicity of Brooke's critical good-will undoubtedly owed something to the occasion. Any boy would like to make his exit from school on an expansive and generous note. But the two threads of Nation and Death run clearly through the tangled observations, and the most studied paragraphs of the author of the sonnets *1914,* are keyed to the second of these:

> It whispers indeed through poetry of every age, but of late the whisper has grown into a cry insistent and very plaintive. It is one of the keynotes of modern art. From Botticelli and Da Vinci this secret passed into the tired beautiful faces of Burne-Jones women and the sad mystery of modern landscape-painting. It is the spirit of Autumn, of weariness, of decadence.
>
> These "decadents" have no new message to proclaim; only the old one — "Vanity of Vanities." On them comes the realization of many centuries' stored learning and wisdom, and they are too weak to bear it. They have looked on life, on love and beauty, and behind all these, they have seen Death. This is the sum of their wisdom . . . . Always through [their] music and the singing rings a chill undertone, the thought that the rose-petals will fade, and the lamps expire, that the night awaits. Or they are as men who in the Garden of Life have built themselves rose bowers with careful hands, but, in the splendour of the sunset, sit pale and listless, because they have seen the face of Death between the roses . . . .
>
> From this insistence on Death comes their eager sad passion for the things of this life which are beautiful to them. Each moment of life, each shade of colour, is the more precious to them in that it is irrevocable. The sight of a rose or a sunset fills them with an intolerable passionate delight, because they know that this scarlet curve of a petal, and that subtle blending of colours, can never recur.[8]

It is from this base that Brooke veers into his elegaic praise of Dowson. Actually the elegy meant goodbye, for Brooke finished with Dowson just at this point when he finished with Rugby. He had only begun his study of death.

---

8. These critical papers are preserved at King's College. Some are reprinted and discussed in Hassall, *Prose of Brooke,* and Rogers, *Rupert Brooke* (London 1971).

Chapter Three

KING'S COLLEGE, CAMBRIDGE

Like its sister at Oxford, the University of Cambridge has traditionally sought to produce capable human beings rather than capable specialists and executives. Both establishments began, some seven hundred years ago, as vocational universities on the Continental mode. Their systems of separate colleges grew up to meet the housing needs of poor young men who hoped for careers in schools or the clergy. But after the thirteenth century, the college system developed as a deliberate attempt to provide promising young men with educational environments which could lead into any kind of career. At Cambridge differences between college and college developed naturally, and were not much controlled by the central system. By the seventeenth century, the so-called University operated as a coordinating group and political bloc, leaving the programs of education almost entirely up to the conscience or whim of the separate colleges. During the eighteenth century, social elitism further corrupted the idea of an educationally responsible central university. By the end of the nineteenth century, the changing requirements of society and government had forced a strengthening of the central University at some expense to the autonomy of the colleges. But the colleges, numbering thirteen in Brooke's time, remained the effective educational units, compared to which the shared units – lectures, examinations, laboratory exercises, the University Library – remained of minor significance.

Brooke therefore entered Cambridge in a general way, but King's College in a specific and particular one. King's itself was a specific and particular establishment. Though not the biggest

1. John Steegman, *Cambridge* (London, 1945), and J.P.C. Roach, *The City and University of Cambridge* (Cambridge, 1959) provide agreeable accounts of Cambridge and King's.

college, it was the most prosperous and most prestigious. One cause of its well-being lay in its possession of the King's College Chapel, one of the greatest glories of European church architecture, and the visual center of the whole University. Another cause developed from the libertarian nature of the King's College charter, a royal document which gave King's, alone among the colleges, virtual independence of the University government, and in most ways of the national government which had become the technical operator of the University. Another was money, for King's had had unusual success in accumulating this substance over the centuries, and retained a good deal of income in modern times. And King's was traditionally, though not formally, connected with the most fashionable and sound public-schools, Eton especially, and also Rugby, Winchester, Harrow — the nurseries of Britain's great men and rich men. From these advantages and others, King's had developed a certain life-style and thought-style. The kingsman, as he was called, was expected to live hard and think delicately. Kingsmen participated, kingsmen were lively, kingsmen were leaders in the group acts of the University and nation. There was additionally a King's way of having mannerisms, though no single prevailing mannerism such as might be found in the smaller and poorer colleges. It was a lively and self-assured college that Brooke entered, but it was also an energetic and competitive one.

At King's, Brooke found much that was familiar and much that was strange. He had existed more under the protection of his parents than was usual among public-school boys, and was rendered a little giddy by the removal of this protection. King's itself offered a set of rules and traditions, and a set of selective preferences which were approaching the status of tradition. It tended to enjoy literature, politics, and philosophy perhaps more than other units of Cambridge. In literature its preferences were modern and advanced; it shared Brooke's fashionable disdain of the Victorians, and participated heavily in the movements of its own time. In politics it was liberal and left-liberal, enjoying the fresh wonders of "scientific socialism" rather than the communist-medievalist patterns of Ruskin and Morris, who were more admired at Oxford. As would be expected in a leading college of Cambridge, King's was extremely interested in the newer kinds of philosophy and psychology. Brooke, like any student of King's, could bathe himself in the happy fluids of speculative reasoning in a position close to the source. Newton was only one of the great thinkers in the Cambridge tradition, while Bertrand Russell was already at hand, and Wittgenstein existed on the horizon. Meanwhile there was philosophical discussion of the most vigorous kind.

In such a setting, Brooke would have been forced out of his merely negative dogmatism whatever the system then *a la mode.* In the system actually *a la mode,* he was swept off his feet. Cambridge philosophy at that time was led by G. E. Moore, one of the most adventurous of modern thinkers, and in addition an agreeable man and a brilliant salesman. Moore's system was just then coming into public notice through his *Principia Ethica* (1905), and Moore himself was on hand and available. Once the contact had been made, Brooke abandoned everything else, and became what could then be called a "Moorist." Seen in retrospect, Moore's ethical system was partly hocus-pocus and partly semantics, and Moore himself a stimulator of thought rather than an original thinker. The system began with a kind of Cartesian solipsism. One could know only oneself, and one's single ethical responsibility was to know oneself very well. One's experience was part of one's self; there could be no question of knowing anything not in experience, and therefore outside of oneself. Within the experience certain events might occur which would suggest the possibility of a cosmos outside the self, some sort of objective reality; but this experience could not be brought to any test of validity. All that could be tested, Moore contended, were certain distinctive "states of mind." For the ideas and images which flitted over the screen of a man's awareness were always accompanied by feelings of pleasure or displeasure, or by both in certain forms and mixtures; and from these an ethical system, and of course an aesthetic system, could be derived. At bottom, Moore's system proposed that the good felt good and the bad felt bad. The system was ornamented, especially at Cambridge, with a good deal of wit, stylistic precision, and wistful allusions to books like *Peter Rabbit* and *Alice in Wonderland.* Leaving out all questions of completeness and utility, it was a most handsome system.

Brooke enrolled himself in the Moorian philosophy much as he enrolled himself in Cambridge and King's. It was a challenge, then a joy, then an increasing entanglement. Among trained philosophers and cool minds generally, systems and demi-systems are judged by consistency, harmony, and formal elegance, like any other works of art. Brooke lacked the sophistication to judge in this way. He looked for "truth," and supposed that one system — Moore's — was "true," and that rival systems were consequently false. For him Moore's unjudgmental "states of mind" triumphantly replaced the Christian religion and the Victorian society. He therefore became not only an admirer of the system but a passionate believer in it, and when possible a missionary. We find him arguing for it in letter after letter and notebook after notebook, and can easily imagine how full of it his conversation must have been. The system invades all his thinking, whether on literature, politics, society, or personal relationships. It touches much of his poetry indirectly, as a general tendency toward the immediate, the experienced, the instantaneously perceived. We shall see how it touches many of his best poems directly, as an absolute identification of instantaneous perception with permanency and value, or of pleasure with goodness.

Whether the Moorist ideas were good or bad for Brooke is an interesting question.[2] They undoubtedly closed his mind to many human possibilities; and when his own personal states of mind grew feverish and destructive, as they did after he left Cambridge, Moore offered no help at all. Nor was Moore's an artistically stimulating system, since it emphasised appreciation over production and pleasure over work. However, it provided a certain mental stiffening for Brooke, and to the extent that it shook him out of his doom-filled Decadent and atheist pendantries it was an important part of his education.

II

The three writers who have had most to say about Brooke in recent years, namely Hassall, Keynes, and Timothy Rogers, had the strongest personal ties with Cambridge and gave the heaviest biographical importance to friendships which Brooke made or maintained in the University. An outsider who contrives to partition Brooke's friends will probably form four separate groups,

2. Bad, according to Dalton. Moore's whole system finds place in *Principia Ethica* (Cambridge, 1905).

each of which was more serviceable and less harmful than the one before. The last and best was the compatible and basically serious collection of young officers brought together in the Royal Navy Division by Winston Churchill under the advisement of his secretary Edward Marsh. The middle group would include chiefly poets, artists, actors, and professional people — Marsh among them — who not only were "artistic" but who actually worked in the arts. The Cambridge group and Rugby group were somewhat merged, and included a few serious young people, particularly Keynes, Denis Browne, and Hugh Dalton, who were part of Brooke's best destiny. But the specifically Cambridge group, which included dozens of bright, inquiring, and literate people of both sexes, had really the least to offer. Charming to know, skilful in talk, aware of their own histories and environments, the Cambridge people were parasitic, and exhausting to have as friends. They drew off much of Brooke's talent and energy and offered little in return.

These Cambridge friendships may be followed through several hundred pages of letters published by Hassall and Keynes. Among them are many names of national significance — Darwins, Stracheys, Cornfords, Asquiths — but few names which achieved significance of their own, even at Cambridge. Local sentiment has made large claims for a few of them. Francis Cornford, for example, is called a poet on the strength of some slight outdoorsy-womansy appreciations, including an epigram on Brooke:

> A young Apollo, golden-haired
> Stands balanced on the verge of strife
> Magnificently unprepared
> For the long littleness of life.

This poem, always quoted by those who wrote about Brooke, is never evaluated, so that the nasty triteness of the first and second lines and the truistic uninventiveness of the whole are never mentioned, and Francis Cornford is never dismissed as the poet-aster she was. There were several Darwins and a young Frenchman named Raverat, none of whom had anything to do, or who did anything. Four Oliviers get in. Brooke was in love with one, Noel Olivier, when she was fifteen and a half years old, and maintained this love for a long time, meanwhile exhausting himself with attentions to all four. There were always Stracheys, in particular James Strachey. It was James's brother Lytton who might have led

Brooke to the Bloomsbury Group and Lady Ottoline Morrell's human collections. There Brooke could have exploited the really significant people: Bertrand Russell, Virginia Woolf, Maynard Keynes, D. H. Lawrence. But the Stracheys were jealous and fussy men, buzzing homosexuals, whom Brooke could not like and ultimately came to hate. His couplet on James Strachey, after Strachey had joined Brooke's group for a camp-out, gives his views quite exactly:

> In the half-light he was out of place
> And infinitely irrelevant in the dawn.[3]

James Strachey was an obvious target, but hardly more guilty of superfluity and irrelevance than the run of the Cambridge friends.

Among the others was a girl, Katherine Cox, affectionately called Ka by the circle itself, and more recently by Brooke's Cambridge biographers. After a somewhat lonely childhood, Katherine Cox had gone to the fashionably advanced preparatory school at Bedales, and then to Newnham College in Cambridge. She differed from the others in a number of ways, being less pretty than most, and also less pert, less vocal, and less demanding. She had a lazy, restful sort of mind, and an interestingly placid emotional autonomy which left her free to lose arguments without being piqued. A kind girl, she became Brooke's mistress because she thought love would be good for Brooke, and in spite of the fact that she was more seriously in love with another man. Brooke, projecting his own personality onto hers, believed that she could suffer easily and deeply, and excoriated himself for making her suffer. Cut off by philosophy and correctness from any direct knowledge of psychology, he never realized that his interest in her was generated mainly by her geometric difference from Mary Ruth Brooke, his very unplacid and unyielding mother. The series of attempts to move himself physically from one of these women to the other, then back, then back again, actually belongs to farce, though handled as tragedy by the Cambridge friends, and subsequently by the Cambridge biographers.

Brooke is perhaps the only poet in the world who, in describing scenes of passion, salutes his lover's "stupidity," and describes how her emotional heaviness flops down upon his airy

3. Hassall, *Brooke*, p. 282, discusses the event.

aspirations. That was Ka. The real love of his life was Cathleen Nesbitt, a young Irish actress, busy and concerned about her own career, and capable of understanding Brooke without leaning on him or making emotional demands. She comes into his story later, after he had finished with Cambridge and the Cambridge friends.

III

One of the attributes of King's College was indifference towards athletics, and Brooke put that part of his life behind him. He still found too much to do. He was early caught up in politics, and as a professed Socialist was gradually drawn "with sweat and tears" into the exhausting work of the Cambridge Fabian Society. Through a series of accidents he also entered the Cambridge system of amateur dramatics, where his constructive abilities were further tapped. Then as a practising intellectual, he belonged to a series of discussion and lecture groups, including the Cambridge Apostles, a peak-prestige group meant to include the brightest men, whether dons or students, in the whole University. As a student he was expected to do a certain amount of reading along the recognised lines, and some disciplined study as preparation for the University examinations of his third and fourth years. Meanwhile there was actual writing to be done, and a regular market to be made in the Cambridge magazines and, if possible, in the journals of London. All this would have made a difficult program even for a methodical and self-disciplined man. For Brooke, who threw out his talents and energies with feverish enthusiasm, it was exhausting.

Brooke's labors as a Socialist are well recorded not only in his letters and diaries of the time, but in the surviving thick sheaf of yellowing pamphlets, programs, agendas, and minutes of meetings. Socialism early took an emotional tone for him, since one of the requirements of the Fabians was that he "sign the *Basis,*" and the *Basis,* or pledge, contained a good deal of material he did not believe in. His own copy of the *Basis* — actually Sidney Webb's volume entitled *The Basis and Policy of Socialism* (1908) — became a repository for loose sheets in which he recorded his own agreements and objections. On the subject of "emigration," for a single example, he jotted —

Small holdings pay best economically.
Revival of Forestry. S. Holdings must have *cooperation.*

But not now true, hand land over *gradually*.
Find out conditions in Denmark and Russia.
18/ [shillings] + prod. of garden + lowness of rent =
   23/ or 24/ in town.
Moves ∵ chance to rise, less dull
In Denmark not dull they stay. In Sweden dull they go.[4]

This kind of speculation went on over the whole of the period of Cambridge, and accompanied such other labors as long political tours with speeches at the various stumps, and the ultimate Presidency of the Cambridge Fabians, with responsibilities that ran from official welcoming of visiting Socialist leaders to preparation of the grim gray programs and pamphlets.

For a while Brooke may also have thought of putting Socialism into poetry. Lord Dalton asserts that a "Socialist epic" his friend designed at this time was expected to show the "final triumph" of justice and equity in social arrangements, but this epic does not survive even as a design. According to Dalton also, the final lines of Brooke's love-poem "Second Best" alludes to the same hope:

> Yet behind the night
> Waits for the great Unborn, somewhere afar,
> Some white tremendous daybreak. [5]

This poem, however, seems mostly to derive from Brooke's own earlier conclusions to the prize-poems on the pyramids and the Bastille. A couple of efforts that remain in manuscript do take up social questions. One is an ironic parody of Kipling's "Recessional":

> But Oh! If any be misled
>   To say we'll share the fate of Rome,
> Or turn from painting the map red
>   To prattle of the poor at home:
> Lord God of Empire turn, we pray,
> Another way, another way.

Another item reduces political oratory to the form of a sonnet. Beginning "Comrades, to Arms! ", it claims that "the Right" —

> . . . gathers fresh warriors in the wilderness.
> And though we all fall, truth falls not;

4. Brooke Papers, King's College.
5. "Lord Dalton's Memoir."

It shatters the fetters, the bolts, and the bars,
And sends an army to the war again.[6]

Brooke worked very hard on this sonnet, as shown by his dia-
grammatic sketches of its prosody on the reverse side of the
handscript page. But he was dissatisfied, and left the poem unpublished.

Brooke's work in drama was both participatory and administrative. It had, moreover, a certain philosophic depth, going as
deep anyway as G. E. Moore's philosophy would let it. It began in
a practical way, when Brooke drifted into a rehearsal of the
Eumenides of Aeschylus, and was asked to participate as an actor.
He proved a bad actor, and was reduced to the non-speaking role
of Herald. An unsympathetic don recorded that he played even
this part with a "glassy stare." He was also noticed by another
spectator, Edward Marsh, who was destined to become his best
friend. Marsh formed the different impression of "a radiant,
youthful figure in gold and blue and red, like a page in the
Riccardi Chapel."[7] From this merely decorative beginning Brooke
became an important and much-employed force in the dramatic
programs of the University. At that time, the Cambridge groups
were committed to Greek tragedy and modern farce, with little in
between; and the decision of a few individuals to perform an
Elizabethan play, Marlowe's *Doctor Faustus,* led to the organiza-
tion of a new group, the Marlowe Dramatic Society. Brooke threw
himself into the new effort with his usual enthusiasm. He played
the important part of Mephistopheles in the play, took a leading
hand in the arrangements for it, and was a key figure in the work of
the society until he left Cambridge in 1910. In his other important
rôle, he played the "Attendant Spirit" in Milton's masque of
Comus.

Brooke's work as actor and manager was understructured by
work as a creator and thinker. Under Milton's influence he began
his own masque, a work of uncertain title which was to be set in
Cambridge and peopled by Pan, Apollo, Aphrodite, some comic
clergymen and parents, and "Faith, Hope, and Charity, as aunts."

6. Brooke Papers, King's College.
7. Edward Marsh, "Memoir," in Brooke, *The Collected Poems* (London, 1918), p. xxiv.

As Milton might have desired, at least when at Cambridge, it was full of the Spirit of the Place. But it was silly too:

A: Phoebus, whose ear the wanton waters lave,
And Lady Luna, Hespereus, the crowd
Of minor astres heavenly lights, with what
Of local godhead haunts this bosky dell — —

B: Am I intruding?

A: No, sit near
And talk: I'm tired of talking to myself.
I always have to shout, being deaf and distant.

B: I'm going in ten minutes.

A: Why?

B: To dinner.
There's company coming out to dine tonight
From Cambridge: the Church Congress. . . .
Deans and Archdeacons, Bishop and semibishop,
Intelligent laymen, suffragens, and wives.[8]

The waste becomes obvious when it is seen that Brooke had by this time hit a certain level of maturity in his honest poetry.

Meanwhile he was veering into dramatic theory. An isolated fragment on King's College letterhead, perhaps written in 1908, shows one result: "Plays," he avouches there, "are to produce certain good situations, given an audience, and performance, of more or less a fixed kind. The more definite the easier to get great things, but the freer the greatly affected [sic] people." What is drama? "Sensations of various kinds." Is tragedy highest, as thought from the time of Aristotle? "Do not *assume* that the highest are all one kind." In a sterner effort, as part of an unpublished "Dialogue on Art," he tried to bring drama under the "states of mind" of G. E. Moore:

> People . . . discuss art . . . in that condition of inability to argue on the subject with any clear beginnings, common assumptions, or hope of reaching the truth . . . . Reflect, then, on what your states of mind are, when you're in front of a picture, or hearing music, or reading . . . . *Macbeth* derives its excitement by . . . complex states of mind [which it] excites . . . . I don't think it can be held that any state of mind in seeing a play is like that in hearing Bach . . . . When the emotions are good, there is nothing more to be said, or done, except to see which are the best.

8. Brooke Papers, King's College.

The paper continues in this way for quite a long while, with the opposite forces of principle and preference dragging each other back and forth among Brooke's own states of mind. He was never going to be a philosopher.

Chapter Four

CAMBRIDGE POET

Almost as soon as he had moved into King's, Brooke had a long conversation with the editors of the *Cambridge Review*. The *Review* was a University journal, but not a student journal. It relied on contributions from a very wide segment of literate humanity, and had a national rather than a University readership. For Brooke it offered a handy means of transition between student writing and mature literary journalism. The conversation was fruitful, and Brooke became a regular reviewer and an occasional reporter for the publication. As usual, he was noticed as a person of high potential, and soon became a member of the governing board. In his third year he was asked to become chief editor, and might have accepted this honorable position had his tutor not protested.

His reportorial contributions of this period, 1906-1909, amount to forty items. Most of these are book reviews; some are notices of meetings, lectures, and dramatic performances. There may have been an idea of his doing belles lettres alone, but his subjects soon spilled into politics and general intellectual affairs. At the outset, he excitedly abused the critical function. His first assignment was to review "great slabs of minor poetry," or more specifically, seven volumes by unknown authors; and he damned all seven with the humorous abuse which is one of the fixed mannerisms of British undergraduate criticism. One mean transitional sentence, "It is a relief to turn from the merely silly to the merely dull," adequately represents the review as a whole. Perhaps guiltily, he said in a private letter that the seven books were "all the same, and all exactly the stuff I write." This was the most sadistic of his reviews in the three-year period, though later, when reviewing a volume of the distinguished *Cambridge History of English Literature,* he was able to attack its professorial contributors with equal cruelty.

The strictly literary reviews expand backward in a rather

interesting way. As his sympathies widened beyond the Decadents, Brooke took on books of scholarly and antiquarian interest. Except for Browning the great Victorians interested him very little, and the Augustans not at all, but he found himself at home with the Romantics, especially Keats, and gradually reached outwards to include the Elizabethans on one side and the strictly serious moderns on the other. He went on liking outsiders. One of his best short reviews reveals a thoughtful appreciation of John Clare's poetry, which had been re-edited by Arthur Symonds. Another deals fairly but skeptically with the last poems of his old favorite George Meredith. The perfunctory short notice which he gave to the *Oxford Book of French Poetry,* the work of his friend St. John Lucas, helps to clarify his abandonment of the whole system of Decadence, whether French or English. Several reviews of Elizabethan scholarship marked his increasing attention to the native tradition, and moreover gave him a little of the language of scholarship, something he was soon to require. His review of Ezra Pound's book *Personae* is admiring, monitory, and critical in the best sense. Brooke never believed in *vers libre,* and deplored "the dangerous influence of Whitman," wherever it occured. In Pound he also deplored "the posing, the unnecessary assumption of a twisted Browningesque personality," calling it "exceedingly tiresome," as many have called it since. The key sentence of this review is neatly balanced; he finds Pound "blatant, full of foolish archaisms, obscure through awkward language not sublety of thought, and formless"; but finds that Pound "tastes experience keenly, has an individual outlook, flashes into brilliance occasionally, and expresses roughly a good deal of joy in life." Pound is serious. "It is important to remember his name," Brooke wrote, in 1909. "He may be a great poet."[1]

In his reviews of poets, Brooke paid exact attention to technique. An amusing set of notes in his copy of R. M. Alden's manual *An Introduction to Poetry* (1909) shows his special and sometimes waspish concern with such things. Actually the book is well written, thorough, and sensible in its approach. Brooke could develop no organized attack, and his marginal notes and underlinings show interest and approval in many areas of theory and

---

1. For locations of all of Brooke's printed reviews, see Keynes, *Bibliography of Brooke,* pp. 103-08, 110-114.

strategy. But he believed Alden's applications parochial and overmechanized, and could not forget that the author was a professor and an American. Alden's careful analysis of meter draws the wrongheaded comment, "We're not to suppose that we read each foot in just the same fraction of a second all the way through the poem? " Alden gave the word "ironed" as an example of "the long syllable," and Brooke responded "Oh! Oh! " One of Brooke's vehement comments occured at Alden's statements about "syllables so grouped as to form a verse." Brooke rejoined, "But what of the Line? " Then, noticing the obvious, he added, "but no doubt he means line when he says verse." Where Alden seems to undervalue short-line quatrains, Brooke writes "My God! " Other usages and assertions are met with "Oh! ", "Ha! ", "Fool! ", "really? ", "! ! ! ", and "? ? ". Alden's observations on drama attracted especially close attention, since Brooke had by this time developed a general theory of drama. Especially objectionable to him are Alden's accounts of act-scene divisions and the pleasure-pain system through which we enjoy the violent and the tragic. Alden followed Aristotle rather than G. E. Moore, and one sees from the various lines and squiggles that Brooke wanted to find something about "pleasurable states of mind" rather than something about "pleasures." In one place, Brooke does make his predilection clear. Alden had suggested that poetry began because of the desire of poets to create adequate representations of their experience, whether inner or outer. Brooke glumly objects, "Is it philosophical to judge what poetry *is* by what the poet *feels* when he writes it? " And he adds, alluding to an issue both Conservative and American, "I suppose it natural to attach over much importance to the producer, in a Tariff Reform country."[2]

This is clever, and would conclude a destructive review with charm and significance. But Brooke sensibly drew back from a specific attack on a career professor whose knowledge might prove superior to his own, and did not go on with the review. In political matters he was less scrupulous. As usual, he tried for combinations. Discussing Granville-Barker's lectures on "Poetry and Drama," he found a good deal of matter which was to influence his own eloquent paper on "Democracy and the Arts." Previte-

2. Alden's textbook with Brooke's annotations is in the Library of King's College.

Orton's influential book *Political Satire in English Poetry* offered an opportunity to discuss both politics and poetry, and may have stimulated the series of satirical poems which Brooke wrote at this time but did not publish. In a charitable interlude, he elected to review a muddling book by his uncle C. C. Cotterill, *Human Justice for Those at the Bottom from Those at the Top.* Cotterill had taken the common Socialist positions on the results of capitalism. Wealth was irrationally and unfairly divided; the rich had prospered at the expense of the poor; equitable redistribution was required; failing this, England would suffer a violent revolution. On the means of redistribution of wealth Cotterill was strictly independent. As summarized by his nephew, his remedy lay in "a plan by which the very richest should instantly and voluntarily come to the help of the very poorest in the land, since both owe their condition to the same cause, the modern commercial system." Brooke seconded his uncle on evils of capitalism and class war ("infinite meanness... the vulgarest warfare ever urged"), but saw the futility of an appeal to the good will of "those at the top" for a sharing of wealth and power. He therefore cited not the wisdom but the moral earnestness of his uncle. "The splendid atmosphere of faith and idealism" and "the spirit of love and an earnest faith in human goodness" are praiseworthy, and he praises them.[3] Of the practical possibilities he says nothing at all.

II

In her generous posthumous comment on Brooke's skills, Virginia Woolf said —

> He had read everything, and he had read it from the point of view of a working writer. In discussing the work of living authors he gave you the impression that he had the poem or story before his eyes in a concrete shape, and his judgments were not only very definite but had a freedom and a reality which mark the criticism of those who are themselves working in the same art . . . To work hard, much harder than most writers think it necessary, was an injunction that remains in memory.[4]

Behind the poems that he actually published there often lay a

3. *Cambridge Review,* May 28, 1908.
4. *Times Literary Supplement,* August 8, 1918.

good deal of study, recorded in notations, notebooks, and private letters. In Cambridge just as before and after, he carefully jotted down things which might be useful. Often he actually used these things, as when an isolated line, "And I am come into my heritage," moved from its position in an early notebook to become the last line of "The Dead," one of the *1914* sonnets. But often they were never drawn forth, and remained merely part of his experience and knowledge.

His notes might occur as lists of words, of situations or plots, of memorable incidents from reading or experience, or of imagery likely to be of use. *Viz* –

Samhain	Sowin
Scathniamh	Sacn-nee-av
Sc-eolan	Scolann
Searbhan	Sharouann

A loves B wholly
– – – – C rather
Yet A is inspired by C, not B.

A story [noticed by Hazlitt] in one of the early jest-books of a fellow who was led to execution, and who, instead of the usual neck-verse, cried out "Have at you, daisy that grows yonder," and leapt off the ladder.

Till the – – – – – rain
And a woman shrilling woke me again
Till I woke again
To a woman singing & the splash of rain

These books are mostly mine. They teach you scorn
Of the Absolute Truth. – Great God, I'd rather be
A Moorist nurtured in Reality
So might my states of mind be less forlorn.

and his little mouth bepuckered in a red fantastic O
I never knew that death could be so mean/homely

Throw up the sole, and then throw up the soul

The night that you were gone from me

man's pride man's pride
I waked alone & wearily.[5]

Other verse and verse materials of the three years turn up in Brooke's letters. Included are squibs, parodies, narrative poems, and a series of personal messages. Many of them combine his technical studies and his personal discoveries. To express "the Sense of Incompatibility between the Self and Universe", he wrote,

> Things are a brute
> And I am sad and sick;
> Oh, you are a Spondee in the Fourth Foot
> And I am a final Cretic.
> Things are beasts
> Alas! and Alack!
> If Life is a succession of Choreic Anapests,
> When, O When, shall we arrive at the Paroemiac.

As ever, he likes to spoof metrical lapses for comic effect:

> Professor Weissman
> Can hardly be a nice man,
> If he thinks that to be a Blakeian mystic
> Is merely a recessive Mendelian characteristic.

This was sent to Keynes, whose ignorance of poetry and seriousness about science always amused Brooke. Foreigners were always amusing; and from "Belgium (a flat country)" he packed his erudition into "Home Thoughts from Abroad":

> By George! I do not like a foreigner
> He is green and grey as sea water
> Unfascinating is the face of him (or her)
>   (Chorus.) By George
>   (Minor Chorus.) Bibble.
> Nebuchadnezzar and Asshur-banipal
> Kosh Lusho, & John K. Billings, were foreigners all
> And now of them, what memorial? [6]

His moralism would never quite die. Noticing the defects of pure autonomy, whether gotten through "Moorism" or mere irresponsibility, he composed a serious piece of parody in an "Anti-Nature

5. All from the Brooke Papers, King's College.
6. Hassall, *Brooke,* pp. 105, 155, and Brooke Papers.

Poem on Railroad Tracks Upon Which I Suddenly Came When Walking on the Edge of Dartmoor." This began "O straight and true! Straight and true! " and continued the stanza,

> For no laws there be in Sky and Sea,
> And no will in the wayward wood;
> Nor no states of mind in the Gypsy wind,
> − − The which alone are good.

The vein of straightforward traditional morality which is only glanced at here was to become decisive in Brooke's thinking a little later.

The longest of these lively experiments was called *The Romantic History and Surprizing Adventures of John Rump. John Rump* is a mixed enterprise, partly prose and partly verse, partly an attack on Brooke's parents and partly an attack on the British middle classes. Its form is masque-like but with narrative prose-passages, so that Hassall could discuss it as a "novel" and Rogers as a drama. The composition begins in Heaven, where God presents the unrealized idea of John Rump with the alternative of existing or not existing, and Rump chooses the former. On earth Rump becomes a Rugby schoolmaster by occupation and an English Gentleman by preoccupation. As a schoolmaster he has managed a House, and skimped on food and heat to make up for his sloppy and inefficient management. His idea of the function of a schoolmaster is "to prepare the boys for confirmation and turn a blind eye on sodomy." His wife has suited him, being lean and officious, "a peculiar mixture of irritable discontinuous nagging and shrill incompetence." Rump's life was gross, mindless, and presumptuous, and his death was physically disgusting:

> ... a fat, restless, sweating figure in bed, the dumpy body swollen and rotted by years of flesh-eating, alcohol-drinking, and lack of any self-control, tossing about in the clammy sheets; the weak mouth slobbering in childish impotence over the bristly chin; the fingers clutching and the eyes fretting with discomfort and a vague babyish fear. ... No awe or pomp of dying; but worry, heat and tangled bed-clothes; an incompetent doctor and tired-eyed, gulping relations; injections of oxygen and God knows what; and, bared of gentility, John Rump, blue-lipped, fighting for breath, helpless and pitiable. ...

> He might have been a thousand splendid things. He was − an English Gentleman.

This description would arise to haunt Brooke two years later, when William Parker Brooke died of a blood-clot in the brain under similarly ugly circumstances. But the fictional English Gentleman is not through yet. The final scene is in Heaven, where choruses of angels wait with God for the arrival of Rump. He is asked, when he arrives equipped with his top-hat, "hideous black clothes," and umbrella, what "splendid tidings" he brings with him from Earth:

RUMP:

    God, I have been an English Gentleman.

GOD:

    Infinite splendour has been in your power;
    John Rump, what have you got to show for life?

RUMP:

    God, I have been an English Gentleman.

GOD (*rising angrily*):

    Was it for this we sent you to the world,
    And gave you life and knowledge, made you man,
    Crowned you with Glory? You could have worked and laughed,
    Found infinite beauty in a leaf or word . . . .
    – – Perish eternally, you and your hat!

RUMP (*not wincing*):

    You long-haired aesthetes, get you out of heaven!
    I, John Rump, I, an English Gentleman,
    Do not believe in you and all your gushing.
    I am John Rump, this is my hat, and this
    My umberella. I stand here for sense,
    Invincible inviolable, eternal,
    For safety, regulations, paving-stones,
    Street lamps, police, and bijou residences
    Semi-detached.

He is also for "comfort, content, prosperity," and tariff reform. As he tells God about these advantages, God dies and the whole seraphic multitude fades off into nothingness. "John Rump remains, still and expressionless, leaning on his umbrella, growing larger and larger, infinitely menacing, filling the universe, blotting out the stars."

John Rump has a number of literary ancestors, and does not express much that is not expressed by every generation as it begins its struggle with the generation just before. Brooke never considered publishing it, though he did read some or most of it to the Apostles at a meeting. He would undoubtedly have agreed to any objections about its failure to grasp the realities of maturity and social responsibility. However, the production is important as a step in his program of the Cambridge years. In its registering the full disgust he felt for his parents, it is important to any analysis of his mind and emotions.

III

During the period 1906-1909, his years as a Cambridge poet, Brooke finished at least sixty poems. Almost half of these found their way into print, and Brooke judged about a third of them suitable for inclusion in the *Poems* of 1911. Had he made another gathering in 1913 or 1914, when his critical views, like his poetry, had grown more mature, he would have selected still fewer. The difficulty would have lain in the bookish and derived nature of many of these poems. Happily, in the Cambridge years he had continued to put distance between himself and the Decadents. But he was left with the great stream of British poetry, and particularly with the Victorians; and in poem after poem he was betrayed into seeking the effects which Tennyson or Arnold or Rossetti had gotten through use of the techniques they had employed, and consequently prevented from developing an attitude or a voice of his own. His large debt could manifest itself in many ways – in false sublimity, in false simplicity, and in falsely catastrophic events, to name only three.

Sublime expression, the first of the three borrowed notes, carried over from the Rugby period with some technical improvement but no basic change. It rushes into almost any opening, sometimes through automatic insertion of tinsel words like "mad," "scarlet," "God," and "eternity," and sometimes as whole images, comparisons, and actions. In "My Song," for example, Brooke begins with a vehement rejection of "sad whining moods" in love situations, but over-reacts to "mad longing," stars that "dance merrily," and winter woods which react to his love so sympathetically as to "burgeon into Spring." Then he skips to death:

> Yes, in the wonder of the last day-break
> God's Mother, on the threshold of His house,
> Shall welcome in your white and perfect soul,

Kissing your brown hair softly for my sake;
And God's own hand will lay, as aureole,
My song, a flame of scarlet, on your brows.

Brooke saw how wrong this was, and did not reprint the poem. In "Sleeping out: Full Moon" (1908), which has a better beginning, he again slips into borrowed marvels:

We have slept too long, who can hardly win
The one white flame, and the night-long crying;
The viewless passers; the world's low sighing
With desire, with yearning,
To the fire unburning,
To the heatless fire, to the flameless ecstacy! — —

Helpless I lie
And around me the feet of the watchers tread.
There is a rumour and the radiance of wings above my head,
An intolerable radiance of wings — —

. . . And radiant bands
The gracious presence of friendly hands,
Help the blind one, the glad one who stumbles and strays,
Stretching radiant hands up, up, through the praise
Of a myriad silver trumpets, through cries,
To all glory, to all gladness, to the infinite height.

His struggle to speak naturally, and his failure after the seductive phrase "helpless I lie," are very clear here. Just so in the two "Choriambics' poems, in "Oh Death will find me," and in "The Call"—

Out of the nothingness of sleep,
    The slow dreams of Eternity,
There was a thunder on the deep,
    I came, because you called to me.

I broke the Night's primeval bars,
    I dared the old abysmal curse,
And flashed through ranks of frightened stars
    Suddenly on the Universe!

. . . I'll break and forge the stars anew,
    Shatter the heavens with a song;
Immortal in my love for you.

He will, among other things "write upon the shrinking skies / The

scarlet splendour of your name." Imagery like this had no con-
ceptual or semantic basis for Brooke, a youth of the twentieth
century, and neither a mystic nor a madman.

But the contrary fault, false simplicity, was equally without
a base for him. A sophisticated son of Rugby, Cambridge, and
much reading, does not convincingly focus his universe, as in
"Song" (1907), down to a cottage dooryard and a spray of
blossoms:

> But — suddenly you, in white and blue,
> By the cottage door,
> And the blue and white of April weather,
> And the apple-bloom — just these together
> I'll see no more, no more.

Nor can he make anything reasonably convincing out of the
mincing complaints of little children against the wickedness of
God, as he tried to do in the "Song of the Children in Heaven"
(1907):

> We were so good, the Angels say,
> That now God lets us sit upon
> The golden floor of glassy stone
> . . . And when a baby laughs up here
> Or rolls his crown about in play
> There is a pause. God looks severe;
> The Angels frown, and sigh and pray.

In the song beginning "Oh! Love" (1909) he begins with a stretch
upwards toward the familiar sublimity:

> "Oh! Love", they said, "is King of Kings,
> And Triumph is his crown.
> Earth fades in flame before his wings,
> And sun and moon bow down. . . ."

Love for "them" is a "crown of thorns" and "vinegar" — porten-
tous and fatal. "I" is not "they," and takes the more natural view
that love is a natural function. But "I" slips below nature, and is
mincing again:

> And so I never feared to see
> You wander down the street,
> Or come across the fields to me
> On ordinary feet.

For what they never told me of
And what I never knew,
It was that all the time, my love,
Love would be merely you.

All the promise lies in the one good phrase, "on ordinary feet." Combined into an absolute new experience, such a tension between grand and mean could become interesting. A poem called "The Vision of the Archangels" (1906) presents "a little dingy coffin, where a child might lie / It was so tiny," carried in state by four archangels "With quiet even steps, and great wings furled." The visual paradox takes on life when the angels drop the little coffin into space and we discover, as it falls out of being and experience, "therein, / God's little pitiful body lying, worn and thin." The poem does not explain itself entirely, but its God has surely died, probably as a child-suicide. The sharpness of image and dignity of language support the sublime-versus-simple situation in this poem at least so far as it is understandable. God dies less interestingly in "Failure" (1908), in "The Death of Smet-Smet" (1908), in "Choriambics II" (1908), as well as in some unpublished poems still to be read at Cambridge.

The third effect of bookishness and failure to record real experience was a dependence on a few officially sinister themes and incidents. The three situations which occur most often, and which are presented as important in themselves, are isolation, aging, and mortality. Brooke looks at isolation from every point of view, finding it among animals, pilgrims, lovers, angels, dead men, and God himself. Old age had a particular fascination for him, as something nearly as fearful as isolation, and considerably more fearful than death. In the beginning his preoccupation may have generated from the Decadent writers, particularly from Huysmans, Wilde, Dowson, and St. John Lucas. Unlike them, he placed old age sometimes among the political markers, with religion, responsibility, and Victorian modes of conduct. More often it is mere biological horror, presented for emotional effect. To express jealous rage and hate, he visualized the offending object as old. Thus in "The Beginning" (1907) —

I'll . . . hold you fiercely by either hand,
And seeing your age and ashen hair
I'll curse the thing that once you were
Because it is changed and pale and old
(Lips that were scarlet, hair that was gold).

In "Jealousy" (1907) he gloated over a lover who had married someone else:

> I'm waiting, lover-wife,
> For the great time when love is at a close, . . .
> When all that's fine in man is at an end,
> And you, that loved young life and clean, must tend
> A foul sick fumbling dribbling body and old,
> When his rare lips hang flabby and can't hold
> Slobber, and you're enduring that worst thing,
> Senility's queasy furtive love-making . . .
> Then you'll be tired; and passion dead and rotten;
> And he'll be dirty, dirty!

Of course she will be "dirty too." Full vengeance. In "Menelaus and Helen" (1909) he carries the reunited Greek couple, paragons of the young world, into the same senility. Helen bears "child after legitimate child" and becomes "a scold, haggard with virtue," while Paris becomes boastful, then babbling, then deaf and out of it:

> Often he wonders why on earth he went
> Troyward, or why poor Paris ever came.
> Often she weeps, gummy-eyed and impotent;
> Her dry shanks twitch at Paris's mumbled name.

At the end of this ugly poem, Brooke contrasts the happier fate of Paris, who cleanly "slept by the Scamander's side." Brooke's old affection for death had not been abated. God dies, beasts die, lovers die, death is all around, and far blesseder than old age.

Though generally a blessing, Death is not always presented as desirable. The chanting naked man-animals in "The Song of the Beasts" (1906) are drawn to it hypnotically as something "beyond lust and fear." It offers a cosmological triumph in "The Beginning." In "My Song," as we have seen, it tempts forth "God's own hand." In the two "Choriambics" poems it introduces a sort of half-lit Grecian underworld where attenuated lovers still meet and try to kiss. Sometimes indeed it provided something new and good. The solid sonnet "Oh, Death will find me" pictures the grey and uncomfortable landscape beyond "the Stygian tide," where shuddering ghosts are waiting in "shade and loneliness and mire." Then the girl comes, dead too, and he watches her –

Pass, light as ever, through the lightless host,
Quietly ponder, start and sway, and gleam,
Most individual and bewildering ghost! —
And turn, and toss your brown delightful head
Amusedly, among the ancient dead.

An original and very charming note is struck here.

In two other poems, "Second Best" and the well-known "Day that I Have Loved" (1908, a contest poem) Brooke strikes just the dying fall he was to strike in *1914.* He says in "Second Best" —

Here's peace for you, and surety. . . .
All day the good glad sun
Showers love and labour on you, wine and song;
The greenwood laughs, the wind blows, all day long
Till night. And night ends all things.

"Day that I Have Loved" presents a dead day in the formularies of a dead person, such as the King Arthur of Malory and Tennyson. Tennyson's *Idylls of the King* provided most of the details. The day has been found as a child is found, and made to laugh and sing and dance, but now the "faint hands" of ghostly women thrust its death-barge "mist-garlanded, with all grey weeds of the water crowned," away from the shore.

The grey sands curve before me. . . .
From the inland meadows,
Fragrant of June and clover, floats the dark, and fills
The hollow sea's dead face with little creeping shadows,
And the white silence brims the hollow of the hills.

Close in the nest is folded every weary wing,
Hushed all the joyful voices; and we, who held you dear,
Eastward we turn and homeward, alone, remembering . . .
Day that I loved, day that I loved, the Night is here!

This is a final night, since "There'll be no port, no dawn-lit islands," only "the drear / Waste darkening, and at length, flame ultimate on the deep." There is no Avalon or archipelago of Fortunate Isles for this dead day.

IV

"Day that I Have Loved" is quite a good poem. It succeeds

particularly in its contrast of color and motion with greyness and stillness, not an original contrast, but a sound one which any poet may adopt in a personal, meaningful way. Though not new, the contrast was real, it was experienced. Some eight ot ten poems of the King's College years similarly transcend models and authorites and borrowed emotions, and represent genuine observation and a personal discovery of language. The skills were developing, and Brooke was beginning to make poetry.

The evidence of this development is to be found in isolated phrases and passages for the most part, and sometimes in whole poems. In many poems, for example "In Time of Revolt," "Seaside," "The Death of Smet-Smet," "Failure," "The Pine Trees and the Sky," "The Jolly Company," "Choriambics," "Blue Evening," and "Jealousy," he managed to bring off lines and sentences of real originality and strength:

> This too avuncular officiousness,
> Intolerable consanguinity.

> . . . all my tides set seaward. From inland
> Leaps a gay fragment of some mocking tune
> That tinkles and laughs and fades along the sand,
> And dies between the sea-wall and the sea.

> An idle wind blew round the empty throne
> And stirred the heavy curtains on the walls.

> I saw the pines against the white north sky
> Very beautiful, and still, and bending over
> Their sharp black heads.

> [of stars] All the night
> I heard the thin gnat-voices cry
> Star to faint star across the sky.

> When the great day ends,
> When love dies with the last light, and the last song
>   has been sung, and friends
> All are perished . . . .

> My agony made the willows quiver;
>   I heard the knocking of my heart
> Die loudly down the windless river.

When I know
That you have given him every touch and move,
Wrinkle and secret of you, all your life . . . .

In each of these passages, different as they are in theme, image, and sound, some genuine and serious discovery is given its own adequate expression.

Isolated original phrases are never enough, and Brooke was not yet able to command much more. Where he came closest was in the series of "unpleasant" poems which he now began. "Jealousy," "Menelaus and Helen," and some other poems already mentioned are unpleasant enough, but lack independence and fresh wording, not to say sense and honesty. "The Voice" (1909) comes closest. Its speaker is a little over-earnest about his own quietness and harmony and one-ness with "my" woodlands, "part of the heart of me." But the mood is set with enough authority to make its destruction painful:

And suddenly
There was an uproar in my woods,
The noise of a fool in mock distress,
Crashing and laughing and blindly going,
Of ignorant feet and a swishing dress.

This "uproar" goes too far in the other direction now; the girl's "cheerful clear flat platitudes" get too much attention, and low sarcasm enters. In "Dawn" (1907), where love and sex do not complicate the problem, there is an almost perfectly independent and successful effort. This dawn is seen, as the subtitle attribution shows, "from a train between Bologna and Milan, second class." As Hassall correctly urged, it is the first poem in which Brooke maintained independence and control from the beginning to end, and is therefore worth quoting entire:

Opposite me two Germans snore and sweat.
Through sullen swirling gloom we jolt and roar.
We have been here for ever: even yet
A dim watch tells two hours, two æons, more.
The windows are tight-shut and slimy-wet
With a night's foetor. There are two hours more;
Two hours to dawn and Milan; two hours yet.
Opposite me two Germans sweat and snore − −

One of them wakes, and spits, and sleeps again.
   The darkness shivers. A wan light through the rain
Strikes on our faces, drawn and white. Somewhere
   A new day sprawls; and, inside, the foul air
Is chill, and damp, and fouler than before – –
   Opposite me two Germans sweat and snore.

What Wordsworth called "the sonnet's little room" was never more perfectly matched with actual inner-space than in this revelation from a European railroad compartment. Brooke almost equalled this feat of observation and reporting in "Wagner," a poem written in the following year after a concert at Queen's Hall in London. One music-lover with "a flat wide hairless face" enjoys "love-music that is cheap":

   His heavy eyelids droop half-over,
      Great pouches swing beneath his eyes.
   He listens, thinks himself the lover,
      Heaves from his stomach wheezy sighs;
      He likes to feel his heart's a-breaking.

   The music swells. His gross legs quiver.
      His little lips are bright with slime.
   The music swells. The women shiver.
      And all the while, in perfect time,
      His pendulous stomach hangs a-shaking.

T. S. Eliot liked this poem and imitated it.[7] But in this case, Brooke had yielded to temptation in the last line, substituting fancy for truth in the assertion that the man's belly shakes "in perfect time" to Wagner's music. One doubts that. Brooke's control still lacked firmness and he could still be seduced by what he himself called "romantic devices – devices, that is, which aim at the beauty or power of some single line or part of the work of art, rather than the effect of the whole." Indeed that mastery of control which his Victorian betters could maintain from poem to poem and volume to volume was never to be within his competence at all. But the question of his ability to rise into integrity and independence had been almost settled by the summer of 1909.

7. Rogers, *Brooke*, pp. 14-15.

V

The Cambridge system of undergraduate education embodied a three-year period of supposedly tranquil discovery and self-discovery, punctuated by a series of examinations handled by the University rather than the separate colleges. Of these the most important was the last, the so-called tripos, which was administered at the end of the third year. The results of the tripos determined the quality of the degree to be awarded. There were three regular classes of degree, plus a "pass degree" which represented complete failure. A man's relationship to his college and the University often depended on the kind of degree he took, and the judgment could sometimes determine his whole future.

Brooke's heavy involvement in drama, politics, poetry, and the demanding routines of love and friendship had cut deeply into his energies. In earlier examinations he had tried to substitute wit and irony for solid learning, and been reminded that that system would not work at Cambridge. His earlier examinations had been unsatisfactory. In the early spring of 1909, when the decisive tripos was impending, he was warned several times of the dangers he was running. His response, as recorded in his letters, constituted an almost hysterical rejection of the facts of the matter. The letters are gushing, excited, and often silly, showing his anxiety by their childishness and profusion rather than by anything said in them. Meanwhile he set up a very juvenile adventure, "dropping out of sight" for the five days of an innocent visit to Noel Olivier's vacation house in the New Forest. He did not study, and perhaps could not.

In June, 1909, he received the news that his papers had been placed in the second class, and low even there. His first response was emotional, and under the circumstances irrational:

Stricken by his failure to get a First . . . he went straight to Frances Darwin, who had now become Mrs. Cornford, and was living with her husband in Chesterton Road [Cambridge]. "The colour was drained out of him," Mrs. Cornford observed. "*I* don't care," he remarked [to her], "but it's my people." He went, and came back again an hour later. "This is for you," he said, and handed her a facsimile of the Shakespeare first folio. Was it his mother, she asked, that he was so concerned for? He said it was. "How glad I am," he declared, "How glad I am that mother isn't just a nice old lady."

The practical effects of his failure were also important. He had hoped that a good degree would slide him into a King's College fellowship with no particular trouble on his part. It was the honor his father had gotten, and it would have provided him a secure academic home and a useful stipend. The second-class tripos forced him to seek the Fellowship by other and more strenuous means. Classics had not worked. Under advice of his tutor he abandoned Classics entirely, and set out to establish himself as a scholar in English literature.

Chapter Five

A GRANTCHESTER WEBSTER

Brooke's letters after the Tripos are conditioned by the anticipated reactions of particular recipients. In gross, they show a steadily growing emotional strain, marked by sharp variations between manic enthusiasm and grim rejection, with various degrees of irony covering the areas between. They also indicate his growing desire for some permanent change in his life-style. He was not very clear about the reasons for such a change. His wild round of fashionable activities – camping out, masquerading in work-clothes, moving around in houseboats and caravans, "visiting," and going to exactly the points in Europe where he would meet demanding people – could not yet be indicted as a weariness and a waste of energy. The fact that he was approaching emotional exhaustion, and that his buzzing friends and activities were bad for him, he found not acceptable. The emotional dangers represented by his mother were clearer to him, but he was not yet clear about their catastrophic intensity. Still he knew that something was wrong, and took what seemed a remedial course of action. This consisted of a move to Grantchester, a village two miles west of Cambridge town, but still in view of the Chapel of King's College.

In Grantchester, Brooke lived first at the Orchard, a modest brick house maintained by a retired couple who let out a room and the use of a parlor. From the Orchard he moved to the Old Vicarage, a rather awkward-looking two-story brick house of which he became principal occupant. The Old Vicarage was saved from narrow plainness by its great sweep of porch-roof almost as wide as the house, by its long level garden terminating in tangles of vines and rose-bushes, and by its proximity to the river Cam, which flowed into the neighbourhood as a creek, made pleasant noises as it passed through the stonework of an abandoned mill, and quietly became navigable by punt or canoe. At the Old Vicarage, as at Cambridge, Brooke lived in the middle of English history and English poetry. Grantchester was in the Roman, Saxon, and Norman records, and had been an important stronghold during the battles between Town and University in the middle ages. It had its grey English church of no date, or of all dates, and on the squat church-tower a broken clock the unmoving wheels of which Brooke himself was to freeze still tighter. Chaucer, Milton, and Wordsworth had passed that way and left traditions behind them, and Brooke could swim in a curving wideness of the river that was still called Byron's Pond.

The location of the Old Vicarage was convenient as well as romantic. One reached the colleges of Cambridge easily by foot or bicycle, and almost as easily by punting down the always quiet stream. The railroad station was still closer, a fact that put the Old Vicarage within commuting distance of London, and in the closest convenient relationship to the wide world of which London remained the center. Brooke loved to fancy that by moving from the Fellows building of King's to the Old Vicarage in Grantchester he had moved out of the cultural mainstreams, but that was only fancy.

Grantchester and the Old Vicarage remain important to the Brooke legend from both the biographical and the literary point of view. Brooke's enthusiasm about the location spreads over some two or three hundred pages of his personal letters, particularly those of 1909-1910, when he remained in residence a good deal. However, romantic fancy of a quiet retirement in Grantchester quickly gave way to romantic fancies about the place as the central meeting-place of a bright youth-circle meant to include mainly his own old friends of the Rugby and King's periods. The values assigned to Grantchester by Brooke thus managed to cancel each other out, the quietness and peacefulness of the place being rubbed away by its popularity and availability. Many surviving photographs show the crowd of young people assembled around their host, always in summer, usually at an outdoor breakfast or near a table on which lie a few books or some pages of manu-script.[1] His friendships had become a cult. The pictures do not show that these convivialities were almost a matter of life and death for him.

Brooke's need to seem "friended" and to seem happy grew

---

1. Best photographs are in Michael Hastings, *The Handsomest Young Man in England* (London, 1967), passim.

more compulsive in these years, so that he continued to insist that Grantchester meant peace and repose, scholarship, health, and friendship long after he had given up any permanent residence. Perhaps the only practical advantage of keeping the Old Vicarage as an official residence was that it gave him a reason not to be at his mother's house in Rugby. In Canada two years later, trying to whistle away his insecurity, he used it as a weapon against Canadians:

> I travelled from Edmonton to Calgary in the company of a citizen of Edmonton and a citizen of Calgary. Hour after hour they disputed . . . Edmonton had grown from thirty persons to forty thousand in twenty years, but Calgary from twenty to thirty thousand in twelve. "Where" – as a respite – "did I come from?" I had to tell them, not without shame, that my own town of Grantchester, having numbered three hundred at the time of Julius Caesar's landing, had risen rapidly to nearly four by Doomsday Book, but was now declined to three-fifty. They seemed perplexed and angry.[2]

They may have thought him rude, and his reference to Grantchester, as "my own town" as lacking substantiality. But a Grantchester of the mind is still a Grantchester, and eligible as a poetic theme. Brooke did not so much live a Grantchester life as write a Grantchester idyll. His poem named for the suburban community, the poem of his which is most quoted and admired by members of the two old universities, was not written until 1912 when Grantchester was little more than his mailing address.

II

Brooke's prose work in this period was always critical in the sense that Brooke was willing to take positions, whether on points of fact or points of merit; but it was increasingly scholarly in the sense that it came to involve more study and a wider experience of literature. The published work runs from short reviews through a couple of genuine literary studies to the book-length dissertation which, in company with friendship and good will, was intended to make up for the unfortunate second-class degree, and get Brooke his fellowship at King's. All this work ended quite abruptly in

2. Brooke, *Letters*, p. 501. Another version in Brooke, *Letters from America* (London, 1926), pp. 170-71.

1912. Brooke had won his fellowship by then, and also had swung down into a serious nervous breakdown. By the time he had recovered there were other things to do, and he never returned to scholarship.

Among the critical reviews, a paper on James Elroy Flecker which Brooke wrote for *The Gownsman* scarcely two months after the Tripos is of interest in the light of Brooke's own progress. Brooke and Flecker were rivals and knew it, so that the review is especially delicate and fair. In it Brooke seized the chance to praise his own most salient activities, including his study of prosody which was now of ten years duration. Judgment is always difficult, he said, because appropriate tests of workmanship vary from poet to poet and class to class. A single universal test is valid in dividing "those who can handle meter, and those who cannot," but other criteria are relative. This is a welcome change from the school partisanship, humorous or haughty, of earlier years. The review also contains a reference to "starved and morbid young men," and to the coldness and refinement of their work, which marks another step in Brooke's emancipation from such men as Dowson and St. John Lucas. "Mixed and vulgar emotions" and "mixed subjects" such as "Hampstead Heath, love, death, wind; Helen of Troy, colours, the loveliness of the world – all the jolly things that really move one," are to be praised in Flecker's work. In "The Great Lover" (1913) Brooke himself was to versify these joys of a catholic experience. Brooke's review of a new biography of Shelley by A. Clutton-Brock is more sweepingly critical. Though again careful to locate both good and ill qualities in the book, he let predilections of his own emerge in an almost frantic attack on Clutton-Brock's approach to Shelley "from the point of view of middle age," and on his corresponding view that much of Shelley's social radicalism belonged to youth and might have been corrected as a result of experience. As a young man and a radical as well as a poet and reviewer, Brooke found these views "irritating," "misleading," "irrelevant," "cultural poison." Discovering that Clutton-Brock could "keep his head" on the ultraromantic question of Harriet Shelley's suicide, he went on to allege that Harriet had been "a foolish, pitiful figure who clogged Shelley's genius, had a weak mind, and was temperamentally disposed to suicide." The antiromantic quality of the poems Brooke had now begun to write is presaged in this second part of the review, if not in the early part on rugged age and youth.

Those studies by Brooke which fall under the heading of scholarship were determined partly by his interests and partly by the strategies through which he hoped to improve his prospects for a fellowship. The base of his reading at this time was the Elizabethans, particularly the dramatists. In form his work ran from reviews to prose essays and to his dissertation on John Webster. These studies are generally characterized by sympathy, and by daring intuitive leaps at whole elements and processes in the work of his subjects. His tactics could still recall those of Frank Harris, as when he wrote of Shakespeare's Richard II:

> If we cannot, as a recent critic has done, trace Shakespeare in Richard, we can certainly guess that something of Richard was in Shakespeare. The case of a man by nature, or his present position, averse from action, the mere philosopher or poet, found in a position where action is necessary; this is the tragedy he brooded again and again, with the painful realism of experience, in those later days when the torture of his own tragedy had made him aware of his own nature. . . . At any rate, in this strange case [Richard II] we find the soul of Shakespeare viewing the same world from the same height and place to which it won, later, through the fire.

Brooke had already begun to notice the work of the prominent scholar George Saintsbury. Saintsbury's interest in the science of prosody appears to have set up opposing vibrations. In a review of Volume V of *The Cambridge History of English Literature,* he was nevertheless able to praise Saintsbury as the only contributor who knew how to write. Other "experts and professors of English literature" wrote "uniform lustreless English, with all the faults of journalese — the flaccidity, the circumlocutions, the trite, lifeless, unmeaning metaphors, the interminable string of abstract substances — without its occasional brightness." But "Professor Saintsbury's chapters among the rest stand out like a hippopotamus in an expanse of mud, clumsy and absurd, but alive." Of course this is a defense of his own critical style, which, as he thought, eschewed the slow and obvious in favor of flashing good taste and enlightened bursts of intuition. Neither Brooke nor any youth could recognise the enormous learning that formed the basis of Saintsbury's taste and judgment. But Brooke "accepted" Saintsbury, and only a month later was able to do a friendly review of Saintsbury's *History of English Prosody.*

Scholarship could also be programmed. There was a review of *The Authorship of Timon of Athens,* by E. H. Wright, an effort which led to one of Brooke's most complete attempts at scholarly problem-solving, the long article "The Authorship of *Appius and Virginia,*" published in the highly respectable *Modern Language Review* in 1913.[3] Never printed, but closer to scholarship than anything else he had done, was a half-historical, half-literary essay called "Puritanism as Represented, or Refered to, in the Early English Drama up to 1642." Brooke had been advised to submit such an essay for the Harkness Prize, a University competition which could provide a good deal of cash as well as some reversal of the tripos misfortune. In form, Brooke's essay was as shambling as its title. There is a certain movement from history to the drama, and another movement from a tolerant tone to a bitter and mocking tone. The Puritans of English and American history were hateful to Brooke by the time he finished his essay on them:

> A Puritan is essentially a man, who, whether wisely or foolishly, and whether by reason or from instinct, regards all the things of the world and the experience of life as means. The artist essentially, in so far as he is an artist, regards them as ends. The dramatists could not be expected to sympathise with the Puritan . . . . But they put before us a portrait of excellent comic value; a long, lean, snuffling man, who speaks through the nose, and in a strange, ignorantly biblical jargon. The more open joys of life fly before his darkening presence; but there is the glint of the goat in his eye. Lying, fawning, foolish, hypocritical, gluttonous, he crawls swiftly along a dusty road, pursuing gold and his own salvation, hurrying in tight black clothes, with pursed lips, between unnoticed meadows.

"The type changes little with time," he added happily, twisting the essay to an attack on "the Modern Puritan." For the Puritan survived. "Remove the clothes, the tricks and accent and language, and you will find him far and wide."[4] Brooke had already found him in John Rump, and in different clothes and accents could find him in his mother as well as his father.

In spite of its drifting form, its trickery with scholarly apparatus, and its irrelevancies, the essay on the Puritans won the Harkness Prize. At almost the same time, Brooke carried away the

3. Keynes, *Bibliography of Brooke,* pp. 104-14,locates these items.
4. British Museum Manuscript.

Oldham Shakespeare prize. Meanwhile, not really knowing what was ahead of him, he set forth on his dissertation, eventually to be called — again in echo of its own sprawling nature— *John Webster and the Elizabethan Drama.* The work on Webster became an important part of his life. Throughout the good year of 1910-11 and the breakdown year of 1911-12 he kept it before him as an excuse for freedom and a reason for self-esteem. At last the work became a sort of hiding-place, and offered a neat excuse for his failure to do things of more importance to himself and his poetic mission. And finally the whole thing was a failure, and he knew it and was ashamed.

III

John Webster and the Elizabethan Drama[5] can be broken into two sections, one fraudulent and often insolent, and the other alive and real, though with more affinity to poetry than to scholarship. In actual structure, the book is more confused than that. Brooke had not had any real conception of design when he began it, and had hoped to get it by with a sort of poetically harmonized collection of earlier papers and essays, as though — to use a phrase of his own — a man could create new life by dashing dead babies together.

He maintained this hope even after the book had been judged inadequate as a fellowship dissertation. The exhausting nature of his friendship system, the increasing confusion of his emotional life, and a continuing vagueness and shiftlessness when confronted with the need to work, combined to prevent his handling the old materials with firmness, or his junking them and beginning again. Unable to remodel the book, he set himself to increase its bulk with "no more facts, but ninety pages more epigrams." He could not coordinate the materials: a once-independent essay on Beauty, following G. E. Moore, a discourse on "the Beginnings of Elizabethan Tragedy" which seems to be made of lecture-notes, a quasi-philosophic argument called "The Theatre" which clearly belongs in some other book, and idle attacks on Elizabethan scholarship as conducted by other men.

5. Accepted as a Fellowship dissertation in 1913, as a second effort, and printed in 1916, New York and London.

When T. E. Hulme, in Berlin, told him about some development in German aesthetic doctrine, he pulled open the first chapter to add a burst about *Nacherlebens-* and *Einfühlungsästhetik,* like an alarmed journalist writing against stop-press. Desperate for bulk, and incapable of workmanship, he loaded the volume with appendices, some ten of them, including the ponderous and wrong-headed earlier essay on *Appius and Virginius.* The clawing arguments in this and other appendices stand in ugly contrast to the haughty man-of-taste lawgiving which distinguishes other parts of the book. Brooke added two bibliographies, one including editions of Webster's known or imputed writings, the other every other kind of book. In conception, technique, and accuracy these are highly inferior products, even for a poet to make, and even in that confused period of the bibliographical art and science.

The Preface with which Brooke sought to explain and justify these proceedings has an equal quality of desperation. The magnitude and number of things to be justified enforces upon Brooke an insolence of style which must have been far from his feelings on the matter. There is at very outset the stipulation that if *John Webster and the Elizabethan Drama* is not clear, a more intelligent reading of Webster would have served to clarify it. "I have endeavoured to keep in my own province, and not to trespass on grounds reserved for worthier feet — Webster's. I conceive that there is much that he can explain better than I." In justification of his tucking most of the factual materials bearing on Webster into appendices, he disvalues them and all the scholarship they stand for:

> To explain Webster's writings it is first necessary to determine what he wrote, and also such smaller questions as when he wrote it, and how he came to write it. Such questions, the questions of "scientific" literary criticism, I deal with in the Appendices. I have taken care to get the most probable answers in each case; for there is such a lot of bad logic and fudging on such points in modern literary science, that one always has to go over the whole ground completely for oneself.

Then when these points are settled "with as much certitude as possible," we have the problems of term and concept.

> There are ... points on which it is necessary to have right opinions in order to understand Webster. One must know what a play is; one must know how the Elizabethan drama arose; and one must know what the

Elizabethan drama was. I have given a chapter to each of these points; not pretending to cover the whole ground, or to do the work of a whole book; but endeavouring to correct some of the more misleading wrong ideas, and to hint at some of the more important right ones. These chapters, though not nominally [sic] about Webster, should be even more important to any understanding of him than the Appendices.

The same reasoning could have been used to justify inclusion of almost anything, perhaps a telephone directory or the Book of Common Prayer. It is reasoning against reason, and leads into the startling defense of confusion which makes up Brooke's last paragraph.

It may seem, in some cases, as if I had contradicted myself in different parts of the book. . . . I think I have not really contradicted myself. Part of the business of the earlier chapters is to prevent the necessity of continually repeated qualifications throughout the work. To express my exact meaning on each occasion would have meant covering the page with "in so far as it is possibles" and "I thinks" and "possibly's" and "perhapses"; which makes the style feeble and muffles the idea. I have, perhaps, gone too far in that direction already.

Did Brooke laugh or weep at his own suggestion that "exact meaning on each occasion" is less than the ultimate object of style?

The generalizing chapters which follow the Preface are no better. In particular, the chapter called "The Theatre" is a farrago of phrases and attitudes learned among the Carbonari and Apostles, and especially from G. E. Moore. The real subject of this essay is Aesthetics, and the question it proposes none other than "What is Art?" Following the baby-talk convention of Cambridge philosophic discourse, Brooke experiments with the putative acceptibility of a concept called "Grumph," and places the burden of his argument in challenges like "What do we mean when we say Grumph" and "What do we feel if it is Grumph that we feel?" Responses having been established, the term Art is put in for Grumph, and so the truth emerges. The definition is made, that is to say, from the consumer's point of view; the Moorian "state of mind" at a temporal point of the consciousness is the determiner, a sort of needle which now swings in to indicate "Art" and now away to indicate other things. The term Beauty is cast aside as not definable, or anyway not useful in defining Art. The term Good is retained with its value according to Moore – that is, Good is "the state of mind we are in" when we say "Good." From time to time, Brooke tagged his term Art to give it the meaning of Theatre or Theatrical Art. At such moments he could utter pontifical statements like "A play is good in proportion as the states of mind during the witnessing of it are, in sum, good." Not so silly as not to note at least two lapses in such a statement, he scrambled to limit the term Good by arbitrary and then by introspective codocils. "A performance [i.e. a dramatic performance] that provokes lust," he declares, "would move pleasant states of mind, but not good ones." Ah so? Well, then, "whether the states of mind produced by a play were good or not, must be decided by introspection." To judge a play one must "examine one's consciousness during a play." This is free-floating reverie about philosophic criticism, and very far from philosophic criticism itself. It is significantly at odds with conventional literary studies, since, as Brooke poignantly notices, an old play judged by the "good states of feeling" it may produce will be many plays, the identity of each one being determined by conditions in the perceptive field. A play viewed and the same play read cannot be one play, and a play seen or read by a dozen persons of different background cannot be less that twelve plays. Brooke admits only part of this defect before skipping off into aphorisms.

Taken together, Brooke's next two chapters constitute a historical review of the dramatic forms from Roman times to about 1642. Capsulization in so extreme a degree relies upon prior sympathies in its audience. Brooke feels able to depend, for example, on the anti-clerical tendencies of post-Victorian literary men. Thus he ventures to say that the Roman church systematically oppressed all the fine arts until the Renaissance, and that the Protestant faction took up this oppressive function as soon as possible after that period. "For eighteen hundred years, religion, when it has been strong enough, has persecuted or starved the arts." This persecution, he claimed, chilled the artistic spirit of humans so thoroughly that early dramatic forms conventionally brought into the history of drama need not be considered relevant. Scop, scald, morris-dancing – no. "The point of an art is in the state of mind of the recipient," Brooke said, returning to his crutch. "Certain pleasant and valuable states of mind when we see it, are what distinguishes dramatic art. Only such causes as produced them, or earlier forms of them, are directly relevant to a history of the drama or the theatre. Folk games and festivals, and even folk drama, have, therefore, it seems to me, no relevance to the history of the English drama." But religious festivals oddly do, for the mystery and miracle plays of Church sponsorship are given their usual important roles in the establishment of Elizabethan theatrical modes, and so is the artistic function of ritual and celebration in the very bosom of the art-hating Church. Returned somehow to prominence are scop and scald also, and minstrelsy and folk dance. Indeed, "their importance to the history of the theatre has always been underestimated."

Once past these prefatory chapters, Brooke deals with groups of real plays. He must stick to radical assertions and sweeping judgments, of course, and it is this part of the book which is properly called his "hussar-ride of criticism." History plays he felt obliged to dismiss as "transient, dreary, childish," "silly and without value," "utterly worthless." Romantic comedies he sabres down as "pretty," "vapid," and useable only on the contemptible stages of "girl's schools." Shakespeare alone had been able to transcend the weakness of these two forms, bringing some "imagination and distinction" to the first and casting a "pink magic" over the second. By and large, the years between "the great years of Marlowe" and "the wonderful, sultry flower-time of the next century," which is to say between 1585 and 1600, approximately, are ridden over as a "period of silliness and undistinguished prettiness." Noticeably the word "pretty" has joined "dirty" among his extreme pejoratives. Not pretty or dirty, Marlowe and Kyd are the great heroes of the earlier period, and Jonson and Webster of the later. Brooke assigns these men their merely conventional value, but does so *con amore*. "Marlowe was drunk on decasyllables. . . . How he must have shouted, writing each line of *Tamburlaine.*" Marlowe was youth in a young season, Kyd was death with the world not ready. The writers after them had confused all issues, Brooke thought, until the emergence of Jonson and Webster showed that "Cleanness and greatness were still there." By 1615 or so, as these two subsided, dirtiness and degeneration came on again — "the triumph of prettiness."

In Brooke's view, Fletcher was the principal agent of the dirty new way of writing — "the absence of serious intention, the only desire to please, the lack of *artistic* morality . . . mild jokes . . . coordinate double plots . . . unreality." As a satirist and moralist, Jonson fought these tendencies from outside. Webster's heroic task was to fight them from inside, using the very materials which they had soiled and perverted.

> Serious tragedy seems only to have reached Webster, after it had left everybody else. . . . With him the sinister waves, if they lost something of their strange iridescence, won greater gloom and profundity. After him they plunged into the depths of earth. . . . As the edge of a cliff seems higher than the rest for the sheer descent in front of it, Webster, the Webster of these plays, appears even mistier and grander than he really is, because he is the last of Earth, looking over a sea of saccharine.

Such paragraphs abound in the book, and are what Brooke meant by "epigrams." Of course they mean little as criticism.

IV

When, listing *John Webster and the Elizabethan Drama* in the bibliography of his four-volume luxury edition of Webster, the Cambridge scholar F. L. Lucas puffed it as "the best book for the common reader," he doubtless referred to the chapters actually on Webster. In these chapters, Brooke presented a preternaturally vigorous writer whose salient qualities were desperation, sadism, fascination with death, an incomparable feeling for mental breakdown and moral catastrophe, and a compulsion to hurl women into corrupt and destructive situations. Brooke's writing continues to be pompously aphoristic, and likely to turn away many readers through its vehemence. But the chapters are, as Brooke insists of Webster, passionately alive. Moreover they are passionately sympathetic. Brooke's real concentration on Webster coincided with his nervous collapse. In these years he accomplished a mental and emotional journey-into-hell of the sort well known to Webster and Webster's dramatic characters. And he felt that he felt as Webster had felt.

Brooke's identification with Webster is managed partly at the expense of Webster's contemporaries, and some critics have urged that he credited Webster with discoveries and practices that might just as well have been credited to Marston and Tourneur. Such claims are made particularly in two matched chapters called

"John Webster" and "Some Characteristics of John Webster." In them Brooke continues to be severe in statement and radical in judgement, but his arrogant tendency to base evaluations on shibboleths of taste and background is much less. His sympathies are now with the man, not with theory. Brooke had found something he wanted in Webster. What had he wanted, and found? In the largest view, Brooke esteemed his Edwardian environment to be a sickly and enfeebled final stage of the powerful Victorian epoch, much as Jacobean had been to Elizabethan two centuries before. The sea of saccharine flowed around Brooke too, and prettiness and degeneracy were the tendencies he found most widely spread in the popular literature of his own time. More importantly, he found in Webster a set of emotional discords which seemed to echo in his own spirit. Above all, Brooke found in Webster a statement of the existential meaninglessness and vacuity he found in his own cosmos. In Webster, as he believed, the universe was presented as an anarchic void, in which, however, human functions like self-awareness and self-sacrifice were possible. Therefore Brooke's John Webster was very much a part of the intellectual process leading towards his farewell sonnets and his death on a Greek island.

The women in the case are not hard to find. Of all the significant playwrights of his time, Webster was most concerned with the tragic themes as applying to women. His two doomed *revoltees,* the noble Duchess of Malfi and the evil Vittoria, fornicatress of *The White Devil,* are equally vital, energetic, and masterful, so that they easily bring friends and lovers to do what they wish; and both are adamant, pertinacious, long-enduring, and in the fine sense unconquerable. Brooke's sketch of the canaille-style Vittoria leaves no doubt of his admiration for this rawhide tenacity. "The stubborness of Vittoria's courage" atones for everything else. For Webster's Duchess of Malfi, Brooke's esteem was boundless. "Sincerity of passion" and "unextinguishable courage" are her tone. To Brooke even *The Devil's Law Case,* Webster's confused tragicomedy, turned on the force and autonomy of its tough female characters. The main idea behind this complex play is a curious lawsuit in which the greedy Leonora attempts to prove the bastardy of her own son. Ramifying events are too plentiful, but women are at the heart of them all. The "ordinary dolls" of late tragi-comedy "remain dolls for Webster." But "the lust and grief of Leonora have some semblance of motion, the suffering of Jolanta has an hysterical truth," and the coarse Winifred "has an unpleasant vivacity, a rank itch of vulgarity . . . which reminds one of characters in Webster's two great plays." Brooke, a man growing up in the presence of a tough and intractable woman, was naturally eager to explore the species.

As a chief architect of situations embodying degeneration, shock, and the traumatic forms of pain, Webster also had a special attraction for Brooke:

> Webster had . . . that trick of playing directly on the nerves. It is the secret of Bosolo's tortures of the Duchess, and of much of Flamineo [in his systematic torture of Vittoria]. Though the popular conception of him is rather one of immense gloom and perpetual preoccupation with death, his power lies almost more in the intense, sometimes horrible, vigour of some of his scenes, and his uncanny probing of the depths of the heart. In his characters you see the instincts at work jerking and actuating them, and emotions pouring out irregularly, unconsciously, in floods and spurts and jets, driven outward from within, as you sometimes do in real people.

Webster had, in Brooke's view, the satirist's "habit of abuse." For him, "every character and nearly every speech has something of the satirical outlook." Brooke was also concerned to defend what others called "the gross and vicious realism" of Webster and his fellows. In his role as a liberated literateur, he assailed such responses as "impudent attempts to thrust the filthy and degraded standards of the modern middle-class drawing room on the clean firmness of the Elizabethans." Clean, but sadistic even in the comedy, Webster must "smirch with his special rankness" all the passions of high and low characters. His two special agents of mental torment, Bosolo of *The Duchess of Malfi* and Flamineo of *The White Devil*, are a "very Websterian" chorus. "Their ceaseless comments of indecency and mockery are used . . . to throw up by contrast and enhance by interpretation the passions and sufferings of human beings. They provide a background for Prometheus; but a background of entrails and vultures, not the cliffs of the Caucasus."

Brooke's increasing affection for the concepts of madness and death was also satisfied by his study of Webster. "Webster's supreme gift," he said, "is the blinding revelation of some intense state of mind at a crisis." Instances of madness in *The Duchess of*

Malfi are "pieces of imagination one cannot explain, only admire."
But it is on the subject of death that Webster transcends himself.
Brooke is willing to use "an early concern with funerals" as a clue
to identification of an anonymous play as partly Webster's.
Reaching the tragedies, he is ecstatic:

> It is, of course, in or near the moment of death that Webster is most
> triumphant. He adopts the romantic convention, that men are, in the
> second of death, most essentially and significantly themselves. He can
> express the whole angry, sickening fear of death that a man feels who
> has feared nothing else. . . . . Webster knows all the ways of
> approaching death. . . . He was, more particularly, obsessed by the idea
> of violence at the moment of death. Soul and body appeared to him so
> interlaced that he could not conceive of their separation without a
> struggle and pain.

Brooke's sonnets *1914,* the sonnets that established his fame,
reflect much of this. But Brooke's final praise is for the atmosphere which Webster casts over the whole – an atmosphere of
hopelessness and voided faith, a bleak macrocosm where defeat is
sure.

> The world called Webster . . . is inhabited by people driven, like
> animals, and perhaps like men, only by their instincts, but more blindly
> and ruinously. Life there seems to flow into its forms and shapes with
> an irregular, abnormal, and horrible volume. That is ultimately the
> most sickly, distressing feature of Webster's characters, their foul and
> indestructable vitality. It fills one with the repulsion one feels at the
> unending soulless energy that heaves and pulses through the lowest
> forms of life. They kill, love, torture one another blindly and without
> ceasing. A play of Webster is full of the feverish and ghastly turmoil of
> a nest of maggots. Maggots are what the inhabitants of this universe
> most suggest and resemble. . . . Human beings are writhing grubs in an
> immense night.

In his final sentence he says that though the night "is without stars
or moon," it offers "sometimes a certain quietude in its darkness."
One notices the rhetoric but also the reservation. When the time
came for Brooke to die, he would wish to know it wisely and do it
freely, not in the deterministic trance of a garbage-can maggot or a
Jacobean robot.

Chapter Six

POEMS, 1911

Still in the midst of his problems with the dissertation on John Webster, still prolonging his adolescence through the endless round of visits and trips and "camping outs," still daunted by his mother and always in dread of going home, still in love with Noel Olivier, but meanwhile learning to love Katherine Cox, Brooke began to sort out his earlier poems and write new ones, and to seek a publisher for his first independent volume. There was some thought of having the prestige firm of J. M. Dent publish the poems; and for a while it seemed that Brooke's friend Raverat, who had taken up hand-press work, would publish them in a luxury handset edition. In the end the new publishing house of Sidgwick and Jackson accepted the responsibility. As usual with poetry, the author was asked to pay the basic costs of printing. For Brooke's book these costs amounted to £10, less a few shillings, and were cheerfully covered by Brooke's mother.[1] Putting his friendships and travels and dissertation partly to one side, Brooke settled down to handle the poetry.

A number of surviving accounts, plus the record of his letters and manuscripts, show how Brooke worked at this time. His long years of practice had given him a set of dispassionate techniques, the basic unit of which was composition through accretion rather than flow. A line or a metaphor would somehow arrive, and he would set it down, alone or with additions, postioned to move towards the final form but not actually built out to it. Later, perhaps hours or perhaps years later, he would come back and push the composition a little farther, and so on till it was done. Though accelerated by the waiting printer, this was still his method in 1911. Frances Cornford, who disapproved of his new manner as "over-grand," admired his workmanlike

1. See Brooke, *Letters*, p. 315, note; Hassall, *Brooke*, pp. 278-91; and Keynes, *Bibliography of Brooke*, pp. 30-34.

attitude with its avoidance of the "emotional jargon" of poetasters, and its ability to make techniques seem "more like carpentry." Virginia Woolf (still Virginia Stephen) stayed with Brooke at the Old Vicarage while he was getting the manuscript ready, and in addition to joining him for swims "quite naked" was able to help with at least one metaphor. Brooke had wanted something to express "the brightest thing in nature," and her suggestion of "sunlight on a leaf" was incorporated in "Town and Country," a wryly intellectual love-poem or sex-poem which he had been accreting for months or possibly years.[2]

The mutual influence of Brooke and Virginia Woolf at this time may have been considerable. Though 29, or six years older than Brooke, Virginia Woolf had not yet progressed as far in her career. She was working on *The Voyage Out,* her first book, at exactly that time. She and Brooke had the strongest respect for one another as serious creative writers. As party-line post-Victorians they shared many important objectives. The main one was concentration or focussing of the personality, with its burden of emotion, intellect, and experience, on single moments of new experience which could be caught and held by means of the printed word. Such previous writers as Donne and Marvell would be clear contributors to such an objective; and the strongest contributor would have to be Browning, who in his more relaxed way had caught at "the timeless moment" in thirty or forty poems, and given the conception its solid Victorian name. As Hassall points out, the conception was also in line with G. E. Moore's view of human experience as successively developed but always isolated states of mind, a view all too familiar to both young writers.[3] Since both Brooke and Virginia Woolf liked to exchange ideas, it is certain that they shared their views on such ideas as this.

An interesting further possibility is that these most advanced members of the most advanced young set in Britain helped one another toward that expression of sexual experience which for both ran along the line − opposite, as they thought, to the Victorian line − from physical through emotional to intellectual or ideal. One example will serve. Brooke had on hand a quite long

2. Rogers, *Brooke,* p. 183.
3. Hassall, *Brooke,* pp. 155-57.

poem in almost-closed couplets, a form undoubtedly suggested by its widespread Augustan use in philosophic poems. His own philosophic poem presented something called "Blue Amorph" as the demiurge or original lord of the universe. This demiurge controlled the functioning of all biology, including the human part, and caused trouble by overstimulating the inadequate human members:

> The side is ours [thus, obscurely] who lack the front,
> Belly on belly rolling grim,
> Sleek, imminent, immute, obscene,
> Closing to menace (wing nor limb!)
> From pointless curve, from noseless cheek,
> Tatooed blue, nine-fold, bleaky sleek.

Mystically, he suggests that the principles of physical sex as governéd by the Amorph is identical to the principles which have established and now govern the cosmos:

> Who knows by what [space left blank] shore
> The master Phantast dreamed and strayed
> Till the low light grew strange and more,
> And in the gloaming, half-afraid,
> Against what dim volcanoes' murk,
> He saw the immortal masses stir,
> Frenziedly gather [left blank] and jerk
> Coagulate distinctlier,
> Clutch at their Cosmos, shape and rise
> Stiffening towards unheard-of skies,
> In frozen stream stand stricken, blue,
> Inenarrable?

His conclusion was never fully worked out, but he had jotted at the end of his manuscript some lines that could be fitted in later:

> Un-nippled breasts that will not suck. . . .
> He fashioned thee, he crumbleth thee,
> The light that sheens the shadows, he. . .
> The Penus and the Ovary
> Thy Infant and thy Mater be. [4]

This uncompleted poem was among those brought forward when Brooke was working on the volume of 1911. Of course it would not do, but he drew lines and ideas from it for insertion in

4. From the Brooke papers, King's College.

several other poems. One of these, "Thoughts on the Shape of the Human Body," was composed, according to Hassall's computation, at exactly the time of Virginia Woolf's stay in the house at Grantchester. As published, this second poem has a movement from the dominance of sex-physiology over all things to a concentration on idea and principle:

> No perfection grows
> Twixt leg, and arm, elbow, and ear, and nose,
> And joint, and socket, but unsatisfied
> Sprawling desires, shapeless, perverse, denied.
> Finger with finger wreathes; we love, and gape,
> Fantastic shape to mazed fantastic shape,
> Straggling, irregular, perplexed, embossed,
> Grotesquely twined, extravagantly lost
> By crescive paths and strange protuberant ways
> From sanity and from wholeness and from grace.

Progress is from here to a sexual activity "simple," "perfectable," and "disentangled from humanity," which may, moving to pure idea,

> Grow to a radiant round love, and bear
> Unfluctuant passion for some perfect sphere,
> Love moon to moon unquestioning, and be
> Like the star Lunisequa, steadfastly
> Following the round clear orb of her delight
> Patiently ever, through the eternal night.

Besides its Platonic nullification of matter and its Metaphysical intellection, this shift in the direction of the poem is important as foreshadowing the disembodying tendencies which were later to characterize Bloomsbury. Brooke was soon to part from Virginia Woolf and the Stracheys, and almost from the Keyneses; but the movement here sketched out was to become part of a general anti-flesh movement in his poetry. Without "rejecting" sex, his verse moved toward a fuller, warmer, account of the emotions and thoughts started by sex, and toward a colder assessment of the workings of sex itself.

This was only one of the new developments made by Brooke at this time. As published, his volume of 1911 contained fifty poems, a number suggested by the fifty which, published in 1855 under the title *Men and Women,* had lifted Browning into his

Victorian eminence. Of Brooke's fifty, twenty were segregated into special sections called "1905" and "Experiments." Neither of these departmental labels was meaningful, the only segregative principle actually employed by Brooke being that of merit. Of the thirty poems presented as mature work, some had been published earlier, and several written much earlier. Only half of the volume, or perhaps less, thus represented recent work. Some of the new poems are rather straightforward explorations of sex and passion, others exploit variations of observation in the mode called Metaphysical, and others rely on shock and surprise reached by naturalistic description. Many poems — "Thoughts on the Shape of the Human Body" being one — straddle several categories, and some do not exactly fit to any, so diverse and inventive was the book.

II

Some ten or twelve of the new poems in the 1911 volume place their main reliance on the discovery of love situations or reactions to love. Only one of these is positive or hopeful, and that one is ironic. Called "Success," this sonnet readjusts the situations of Browning's "Porphiria's Lover" by letting a mad speaker suppose that his beloved, through granting "my sick blasphemous prayer," would make herself rotten and evil. Her success, and his, lies in their never having any contact. The other poems of this group divide into analyses of situations in which love is not formally prevented, but does not produce contact, and usually fails to seem worth having. Those earlier mad flaming loves which made the stars waltz and the Trinity stand applauding have disappeared from Brooke's work, never to return.

"The Charm" and "Finding" present a one-sided and blocked-off love in similar ways. Both poems set up night scenes with the male lover awake and miserable while the female beloved sleeps peacefully in the moonlight far away, "beyond the ocean." Some satisfaction is attained through the fact that the distant sleepers are visually available to the speakers, as in "The Charm":

> ... you, asleep,
> In some cool room that's open to the night,
> Lying half-forward, breathing quietly,
> One white hand on the white

Unrumpled sheet, and the ever-moving hair
Quiet and still at length! [sic]

The poems differ in form and tone, but self-pitying sentimentality disfigures both of them. This emotion is picked up in a third poem, "Paralysis," in which the speaker is literally and organically paralyzed, lying in hospital, visited by his "lithe and free" beloved, and then cheerfully abandoned while she moves down a High Street and "beyond the town":

> The strong down
> Smiles you welcome there; the woods that love you
> Close lovely and conquering arms above you.
> Oh ever-moving, O lithe and free!
> Fast in my linen prison I press
> On invisible bars, or emptily
> Laugh in my great loneliness.

Death rather than disease is the separating factor in "Desertion," a poem in long-line couplets which gracefully incorporate many internal rhymes. In "Desertion" the dead girl is blamed for dropping out:

> Was it something heard,
> Or a sudden cry, that meekly and without a word
> You broke the faith, and strangely, weakly, slipped apart?
> You gave in – you, the proud of heart, unbowed of heart!
> Was this, friend, the end of all that we could do?

In dying she failed him. An equally flat idea hidden under learned forms offers a bereaved lover moving upwards towards cool mountain-tops; for he proposes to mourn the girl's death in "clean solitude" while her grovelling family and friends conduct their sticky funerals down below. The title here is "Lines Written in the Belief that the Ancient Roman Festival of the Dead was called *Ambarvilia.*" The form is ballad stanza and the language learnedly over-simple, with phrasing shamelessly lifted from A. E. Housman. The qualities cited in Brooke's "Letter to a Live Poet" as "irregular thoughts in stanzas regular" and "modern despair in antique meters" are competently illustrated here.

Love seen from other angles may be comic or destructive. Brooke handles this proposition in a wide varieties of manners. Sometimes he was sprightly, as in "The One Before the Last." Here, finding himself in a love-agony, he reasons his way out. An earlier passion that was "Hell in Nineteen-five" is only a "faded dream of Nineteen-ten," and the agony of 1910 will be perfectly bearable in 1920, by which time, he mistakenly supposes, he will have a new love with its new agony. In a sonnet beginning "I said I splendidly loved you: it's not true," he declares himself personally inadequate to maintain a great or splendid love. A sounder personality could handle the grand passion with its "long swift tides" and "clean clear bitter sweet" –

> But – there are wanderers in the middle mist
> Who cry for shadows, clutch, and cannot tell
> Whether they love at all, or, loving, whom:
> An old song's lady, a fool in fancy dress,
> Or phantoms, or their own face in the gloom;
> For love of Love, or from heart's loneliness.
> Pleasure's not theirs, nor pain. They doubt, and sigh,
> And do not love at all. Of these am I.

This is a useful catalog of what Brooke and many other romantic young men could and can utilize as love-objects. In another sonnet, "Day and Night," he presents the same concept from a different angle. The poem is set up as a tableau of personified abstractions. In the male's "heart's palace" the female sits enthroned all day, while a glittering retinue of "Hopes" and "Dreams" and "Sighs" and "Memories" swirl around to "worship and love and tend" her. But at night these others "go straying" and the queen herself must exit "out into the night." The enshrining heart works only by day, and its passions are flitting and contrived.

Offered as soberly personal are "Kindliness," a longer poem in octosyllabic meter, and "The Hill," an excellent sonnet. "Kindliness" too obviously plays upon a mere phrase which got into Brooke's head and troubled him, while "The Hill" compresses a lot of his experience into a clear scene. The rankling comfort someone has offered him is that "love changes to kindliness," and he repeats the mean second term over and over. Kindliness is a " lean twilight" and a bad "second best" –

> That time when all is over, and
> Hand never flinches, brushing hand;
> And blood lies quiet for all you're near;
> And it's but spoken words we hear
> Where trumpets sang; when the mere skies

Are stranger and nobler than your eyes;
And flesh is flesh, was flame before;
And infinite hungers leap no more
In the chance swaying of your dress;
When love has turned to kindliness.

Both of the lovers in "The Hill" are young, beautiful, and enthusiastic, and one of them is sensible. They keep insisting on their gloriousness:

We are earth's best, that learnt her lesson here.
Life is our cry. We have kept the Faith! " we said;
"We shall go down with unreluctant tread
Rose-crowned into the darkness! " – Proud we were
And laughed, that had such brave true things to say.
– And then you suddenly cried, and turned away.

Not because of the darkness, obviously, but because of the pretentiousness. "The Hill" embodies a self-doubting wisdom not yet allowed to get into Brooke's everyday thinking.

III

Poems which emphasise man's unconquerable image-making apparatus rather than man's emotional upsets include "The Life Beyond," "Dust," "Mummia," and the developmentally paired "Goddess in the Wood" and "Dining-room Tea." Each of these poems places the heaviest reliance on a major metaphor, or conceit, which is exact, intellectual, and surprising – the qualities appointed to "metaphysical poetry" ever since Dr. Johnson named the form in his *Life of Donne.* Brooke's prime debt was so conspicious in the volume of 1911 as to make James Elroy Flecker call him "our Donne Redivivus" in a review. As metaphor and manner, the metaphysical impulse was also to be found in many poems not in the set. The already-quoted allusion to "the star Lunisequa" which is always to be seen in the neighbourhood of "the round clear orb of her delight," to wit the moon, is a perfectly organized metaphysical metaphor, and the flat analytic tones often employed in poems of the section following adequately present the metaphysical manner. The poems just named have both.

In this group, where the metaphor manages to preside, the source of imagery is consistently visual, and the effect sought has its closest parallel in the enlargements, reductions, stopmotion, diffusion, and special focussing which may be achieved by shutters and lenses. The prime ideal is a striking and original focus brought into existence for an exactly appropriate length of time. In "Mummia," the most learned of these poems, all bookish romance is clicked down to the consciousness of the two liberally educated lovers lying in their bed. "Kings of old" once put the dust of royal mummies in their wine in order to concentrate imperial experience into an aphrodisiac, "to fire their limbs of lead" –

> Making dead kings of Africa
> Stand pander to their bed;
>
> Drunk on the dead, and medicined
> With spiced imperial dust,
>
> In a short night they reeled to find
> Ten centuries of lust.

Similarly, through an intellectual concentration, all the famous lovers immortalized in "paint, stone, tale, and rhyme," can be "sucked" and "stuffed" into one's own copulation "to rarify ecstasy." Helen, Cleopatra, and Juliet, to name three:

> Helen's the hair shuts out from me
> Verona's livid skies;
> Gypsy the lips I press; and see
> Two Anthonys in your eyes.
>
> Woven from their tomb, and one with it
> The night wherin we press
> Their thousand pitchy pyres have lit
> Your flaming nakedness.

He concludes that "the height of the world has flamed and faded" to distill one's love "to this." Moving in the other direction, but maintaining his learned allusions and simple quatrains, in "Dust" he imagines the lovers as "stiffened" and "crumbled" into "motes of dust" –

> And every mote, on earth or air,
> Will speed and gleam, down later days,
> And like a secret pilgrim fare
> By eager and invisible ways;

> Nor ever rest, nor ever lie,
>   Till, beyond thinking, out of view,
>   One mote of all the dust that's I
>   Shall meet one atom that was you.

The conjunction of lovers concentrated to dust particles will produce a "sweet and strange unquiet glow"; and in this warm radiance other lovers, people still to come, will "burn and faint," and at last know "what it is to love." The action of "Mummia" is therefore turned exactly backwards in "Dust," and the inward focussing of great historical regions down to the pairing lovers is answered by the outward focussing back into the sprawl of space and time.

"The Life Beyond," least-known poem of this series, takes its main conceit from Browning's poem "Rephan." In it Brooke delineates the perfect desolation, or desolate perfection, of a kind of life-after-death. Here is the ugly underside of Platonism, with the dead man aghast and horrified at the solid and unchangable condition in which he finds himself:

> No life is in that land,
>   Himself not lives, but is a thing that cries,
>   And unmeaning point upon the mud; a speck
>   Of moveless horror; an Immortal One
>   Cleansed of the world.

Brooke's metaphors do not stay consistent throughout, but the philosophic maxim that a perfect thing cannot possibly change is well enough staged. He makes his personal connection at the very end, when this utter stillness and immobility is shown to match a state "when love for you died." Moving farther into the concept of timelessness, he wrote "The Goddess in the Wood," another sonnet. Here it is proposed that "the lady Venus," standing outdoors in golden morning, suddenly finds all sound and motion stopped dead-still:

> Wing and leaf, and pool of light
>   Forgot to dance. Dumb lay the unfailing stream;
>   Life one eternal instant rose in a dream
>   Clear out of time, poised on a golden height.

Finding the life of the universe as it were frozen, Venus experiences a "swift terror" which starts things going again, so that birds sing and waters purl and the breeze moves the branches. Venus's reactions, which include "flashing" her "immortal

limbs . . . to the human lover" while her "immortal eyes . . . look
on death," seem a little confused, probably because of the unnecessary element of Venus's prior experience of permanence
achieved through divinity. With this element left out, and with a
localization of the landscape and personnel, the conceit of the
frozen moment moved into "Dining-Room Tea," which is in all
respects one of Brooke's finest accomplishments.

"Dining-Room Tea" was written in commemoration of an
actual tea-party at Crediton, in Devon, one incident of a camping
experience which included Virginia Woolf, James Strachey,
Katherine Cox, and others important to the story of Brooke.
Besides the people, the dining-room itself is available to scholarship, having been photographed in all its provincial narrowness
only a little while after the poem appeared, and reproduced in
illustration of several books including Hassall's biography.[5]
Brooke's concern was with the people present, the friends upon
whom he depended so much, and who familiarly appear in the
poem as "you and you and you." With Venus gone, and friends
present, a delicate balance between humor and poignancy could be
achieved. There is movement and sound and tea going into cups,
but suddenly all this stops dead-still:

> I saw the immortal moment lie.
> One instant I, an instant, knew
> As God knows all. And it, and you
> I above Time, oh blind! could see
> In witless immortality.
> I saw the marble cup; the tea
> Hung on the air, an amber stream;
> I saw the fire's unglittering gleam,
> The painted flame, the frozen smoke,
> No more the flooding lamplight broke
> On flying eyes and lips and hair;
> But lay, but slept unbroken there,
> On stiller flesh, and body breathless,
> And lips and laughter stayed and deathless,
> And words on which no silence grew.
> Light was more alive than you.

5. See Brooke, *Letters*, pp. 203, 360, and Hassall, *Brooke*, pp. 283-84 and
photo at p. 288.

"You," a love-word in this poem, means all the intimates whom Brooke thought of as permanent parts of his world and his consciousness. The "mask of transciency" now returns with sound and movement:

> Time began to creep.
> Change closed about me like a sleep.
> Light glinted on the eyes I loved.
> The cup was filled. The bodies moved.

The action is that of resurrection after death in the traditional Christian metaphor, and Brooke would have noticed this since earlier he had actually godded these friends, calling them "august, immortal, white, / Holy and strange." He goes on,

> The drifting petal came to ground.
> The laughter chimed its perfect round.
> The broken syllable was ended.

This was a "timeless end," since through the experience he came to know the "eternal holiness" of these people –

> We that knew the best
> Down wonderful years grew happier yet.
> I sang at heart, and talked, and eat,
> And lived from laugh to laugh, I too,
> When you were there, and you, and you,.

The worshipped friends were not going to live from "laugh to laugh," were not all that admirable, and were not even to stay friends through the next year. An artificial irony comes into the poem when it is understood as Brooke's serious comment on Brooke's own life.

IV

Though its rhythms are lighter, and though it takes its author into a mystic state reserved by the solid Browning for his mad or mystical characters, "Dining-Room Tea" clicks back to Browning rather than to Donne. The poem most used was "Porphyria's Lover," to which Brooke owed some actual phrasing as well as the general encouragement he needed before committing himself to the "eternal moment." Brooke, like Ezra Pound and other post-Victorian poets, also relied on Browning as much as any poet for support in his excursions into shock. In the shocks provided through naturalism, it was often possible to go beyond the master. Neither Browning nor any other poet had handled the righteous jangle of word-oriented pairs better than Brooke did in his short poem "Colloquial":

> It was not that you said I thought you knew
> Or that you thought I said that you, my dear,
> Felt what I felt you felt . . . .

Other poems in which the sensibility of middle-class readers was deliberately flouted included "A Channel Passage" and "Lust," two skillfully composed Shakespearian sonnets.

In "A Channel Passage" Brooke picked up an idea now to be found among his trial manuscripts. One of those never-published scraps bodies forth an overfed idealist whose gluttonies end when he must "throw up the sole, and then throw up the soul." In the more complete system of "A Channel Passage," a lover on a Channel steamer feels queasy and realizes that he "must think of something, or be sick." Since he can think only of a lover who in her way is also unsatisfactory, the contest is between "a seasick body and a you-sick soul." Nobody wins in the end. Physically the speaker disgorges "old meat, good meals, brown gobbets;" and emotionally he has "acrid return and slimy, / The sobs and slobber of a last year's woe." Though the idea existed in the earlier poem, Brooke was brought back to it by a ptomaine-poisoning episode which began in Switzerland during the Christmas season of 1909. He is said to have fainted among the pictures in the Louvre on his way through Paris on route to the Channel steamer. "Lust," the other deliberate shocker, is a sex-poem as compared to a love-poem.[6] Here primitive "wheels of will" catch the speaker and compel him to move, sans mind, morals, and ideas of marriage, towards somebody he lusts after. As the event proceeds, his crowing about "victory" and his "conqueror's blood" shows how brutally the matter stands. A particular phrase which made reviewers and friends squeal was "your remembered smell." Brooke was able to point out in several amused letters that if he had used "odor" as in "odor of your hair" nobody would have been alarmed.

6. See Brooke, *Letters,* pp. 351-16. In deference to his publisher Brooke changed the title from "Lust" to "Libido". Editors after 1915 changed it back to "Lust."

In a somewhat similar poem, "Town and Country," he again carries matters right into the bedroom, though with a difference. The question here developed is whether rooms in the city (as actual) or hillsides in the country (as possible) are more appropriate as backgrounds for sexual love. Brooke's strategies here, and some of his phrasings as well, have a debt to the "Ode on Melancholy" of Keats. Just as Keats warned perfectionists of melancholy never to go to graveyards and old churches, Brooke warns perfectionists of love to stay out of starlight and green country. Conducting an "unwalled" love outdoors, the pair would find their passion dissipating itself among "unheeding stars," "Stranger hills," and other disconnected features of landscape. In the city, on the other hand, a sexy isolation is obtained through the enclosing circumambiance of "straight lines and silent walls," and the "roar, and glare, and dust," not to mention the "undying passers":

> Here, million pulses to one center beat:
> Closed in by man's vast friendliness, alone,
> Two can be drunk with solitude, and meet
> On the sheer point where sense with knowing's one.

The "intensest heavens between close·lying faces" are further intensified by "the lamp's airless fierce ecstatic fire," and would only be diluted among astronomical luminaries.

Both "Lust" and "Town and Country" express simple situations of physical love existing for its own sake, free of the philosophy, history, and politics which like to entwine themselves around the basic couplings. Two of the poems, "Sonnet Reversed" and "Dead Men's Love," stay within the naturalist movement while nevertheless presenting some of these entwining forces. 'Sonnet Reversed" is strict social naturalism. In the concluding couplet of this sonnet we find that the lovers once "stood on supreme heights" amid "amazing lights / Of heart and eye," with "Hand trembling toward hand." But the twelve foregoing lines have shown what Brooke regarded as the horrors of suburban family life, child-rearing, and a business career. "Dead Men's Love ' was unexpectedly pounced on by several reviewers, and called "especially disgusting" and "ribald" by a writer in the *Oxford Magazine,* a journal Brooke would rather have pleased.[7]

7. *Oxford Magazine,* November, 1912.

After a strong line, "There was a damned successful poet," and a weaker second line which contains "a woman like the sun," the poem asserts too confusingly that this pair is "dead without knowing it."

> They did not know his hymns
> Were silence; and her limbs
> That had served love so well
> Dust, and a filthy smell.

The unsuspecting lovers go on making love and dashing around on "the streets of Hell." until they are awakened to the truth by observing "with a sick surprise / The emptiness of eyes." The reader is never sure whether their death is physical or metaphorical. Some details of the imagery display affinity with the poems of the metaphysical group, but here the concepts early grow confused, and finally are lost behind the grittily distasteful details.

V

A well-known poem of Edward Thomas, who was soon to become Brooke's friend, directs attention to the miseries of small creatures like "the lark, the linnet, and the hare" —

> Little things that run and hide
> And die in darkness and despair.

The brightly intellectual social exertions of Brooke, maintained as they were in absence of a secure base such as might have been found in a satisfactory job or family, were becoming burdensome. By 1911, as his letters show, he had become aware of the patchy and scrappy nature of his existence. Meanwhile his old friends began to head towards careers, or to pair off and marry. New combinations were being made every month. He was not in any of them; and yet for many reasons, including his own needs, he was not out of them either. Now, two new and contrary developments began to show themselves beneath the cracking enamel of his well-being. One found its form in several intense poems setting forth the values of solitude through hiding, and the other in a still more intense fancy — called a "wonderful plan" — by which, through continuation or repetition of youth, he could maintain the rapidly disappearing conditions of his young manhood.

The chief artifacts in the hiding-place movements are

"Flight" and "The Fish," the second being also a totally admirable poem. "Flight" is a poem of seven five-line stanzas with meticulously varied rhythms. The speaker is in flight; his "steady paces" carry him past villages and fields and "country eyes and quiet faces;" finally he reaches a vast solitary region of tall pines. In this place,

> I found a flowering lonely bush
> And bowed, slipped in, and sighed and curled,
> Hidden at rest from all the world.

In this "intricate house" he knows himself "safe and glad," but feels himself still endangered, so that he lies cringing "with cold heart and cold wet brows." The thing he has been hiding from now finds him out:

> And silence, silence, silence found me –
> I felt the unfaltering moment creep
> Among the leaves. They shed around me
> Calm clouds of scent, that I did weep;
> And stroked my face. I fell asleep.

Silence may be death, as a permanent form of itself; but Brooke does not go beyond its qualities, which are fearful and horrible, and yet soothing enough to produce sleep, which indeed gives another form of silence. Weariness and fear, moving through silence to extinction, are what the poem presents.

"The Fish" is a marvellous construction of life as it might be experienced by a finned solitary in a slow-moving, green-and-brown, mud-buttomed stream such as the Cam is as it passes through Cambridge. The likeness of the fish's "dark ecstasies" amid "drowned colours" in his "perpetually curving world" to the world experienced by certain sex principles (including the sperm) had certainly struck Brooke and appealed to him. In "The Fish" this likeness is stated, though not insisted upon.

> Silent waters weave for him
> A fluctuant marble world and dim,
> Where wavering masses bulge and gape
> Mysterious, and shape to shape
> Dies momently through whorl and hollow
> And form and line and solid follow
> Solid and line and form to dream
> Fantastic down the eternal stream.

An obscure world, a shifting world,
Bulbuous, or pulled to thin, or curled
Or serpentine, or driving arrows,
Or serene glidings.

The fish lives, conducts his love, and finally dies in the same wet ecstasy.

Grows
An eddy in that ordered falling,
A knowledge in the gloom, a calling
Weed in the wave, gleam in the mud —
The dark fire leaps along his blood;
Dateless and deathless, blind and still,
The intricate impulse works its will;
His woven world drops back; and he
Sans providence, sans memory,
Unconscious and directly driven,
Fades to some dark sufficient heaven.

Brooke's strategy was to emphasize the dark, humid, curving life of the fish (or whatever) by presenting its opposite in the form of noisy and impertinent people on the shore:

Oh world of lips, Oh world of laughter,
Where hope is fleet and thought flies after;
Of lights in the clear night, of cries
That drift along the wave and rise
Thin to the glittering stars above,
You know the hands, the eyes of love.

Also "the sigh," "the song," and other sophistications of love. But this is flimsy stuff compared to the primitive reality of the fish, to which the poem inevitably moves back.

The secret deeps are whisperless;
And rhythm is all deliciousness;
And joy is in the throbbing tide,
Whose intricate fingers beat and glide
In felt bewildering harmonies
Of trembling touch, and music is
The exquisite knocking of the blood.

Like the phallus in the "Blue Amorph" poem, the fish has a cosmic wholeness:

Space is no more, under the mud;
His bliss is older than the sun.

Silent and straight the waters run.
The lights, the cries, the willows dim,
And the dark eyes are one to him.

The poem has often enough been praised as verse.[8] It needs to be considered as an important biographical item as well.

Brooke wrote "The Fish" in Munich, in the early spring of 1911, when he felt deserted and lonely though not yet desperate. He liked the poem and was to work on another version, more brittle and not so good, when he was once again alone in the South Pacific period. Between the two versions he tried to develop his eternal-youth scheme. Had he not left the record in literally scores of pages of private letters, it would be impossible to believe that he took his scheme seriously. As expressed to the chosen participants, it involved going on with "ordinary life" until 1933, when the golden lads and ladies would drop all their middle-class early-forties responsibilities, meet again on a Swiss railway platform, and exit from England, or maturity, or whatever it was distressed them – distressed Brooke, more exactly. A few sentences from the letters will illuminate both the plan and its tone:

> The very splendid . . . class doesn't *naturally* grow old. It does so, in this present world, because of the bloodiness of arrangements. And if people of that class don't grow old – my God how splendid! . . .
>
> We are twenty-something. In 1920 we shall be thirty-something. In 1930 we shall be forty-something. Still running to and fro – London, Petersfield, Cambridge. Still in a country where one *has* to know so many stupid dull stupid grey-lived sleepers. . . .
>
> There've been other people in other generations who swore not to get old, who found Life as good as we do, and vowed to keep it so, to stay young and clean-eyed.
>
> Where are they now? Dead. You meet their bodies walking the streets of London, fat, dead, top-hatted ghosts, haunting the civilization that was their ruin.
>
> Suppose that a band of the splendid young people. . . .
>
> A number of splendid young people, splendidly young together. . . .
>
> The idea, the splendour of this escape back into youth. . . .
>
> We . . . vowing to *live* such an idea . . . reborn to find and make a

8. T. S. Eliot, who praised it, did not notice the deliberate contrast of brittle surface life and basic water life. See *The Egoist,* September, 1911.

new world together, vanishing from the knowledge of men and things they knew before, resurgent in sun and rain. . . .

On the first of May, 1933. at breakfast-time, we will meet on Basle Station. . . . On that spring morning, in that mad place, whiskered and absurd and unrecognisable, we'll turn up. And then?

— Then Life! What else matters? . . .

This is an offer. A damn serious and splendid offer. Take your time and consider. . . . All can be slowly worked out. . . .

It has made me wholly happy about Life. Life is beyond words good . . . . We'll live romance, not talk it. We'll show the grey un-believing age, we'll teach the whole damn world, that there's a better heaven than the pale serene Anglican windless harmonium-buzzing Eternity of the Christians, a Heaven in Time, now and forever, ending for each, staying for all, a Heaven of Laughter and Bodies and Flowers and Love and People and Sun and Wind in the only place we know or care for, ON EARTH.[9]

The importance of such a fantasy, spread over so much paper, lies not in its absurd conditions but in the fact that for many months Brooke worked earnestly at it. His friends did not. If they let him enroll them among the haloed "Persons who are Going," they did so because they did not take Brooke seriously any more, except as a possible poet. But he went on insisting, perversely and alone, that the mission of all the splendid friends was to go on being friends. and being splendid.

9. Brooke, *Letters,* pp. 184, 194, and ff.

Chapter Seven

CONFUSION

The firm of Sidgwick and Jackson spent only £3 for advertising, leaving *Poems by Rupert Brooke* to stand or fall on its own merits. The book was nevertheless well received. Reviewers were in agreement as to its special qualities of vigor, intelligence, and technical skill. They noticed faults too. In the influential *Nation,* Brooke was found to have chosen "unpromising tasks, which demand an athletic vigor and activity." From Donne, the reviewer added, Brooke had learned "to be not only skilful, but to be insolently skilful as well." The *Daily News* noted Brooke's "incapacity for illusion" and detected behind many poems a "bromidinally platitudinous" Dark Lady. Both the *Saturday Review* and *T. P.'s Weekly* charged mental or emotional limitations, a constriction of "outlook on life," and attitudes that were — a term Brooke must have hated — "ordinary"; but found high praise for "his personality, his ideas, his art." Added the former journal, "He already seems entirely able to say all he has to say [and to] vary his manner of attack like a virtuoso on a musical instrument." The so-called "ugly poems" were condemned by most reviewers, who, however, disappointed Brooke by attributing them to his personal anxieties rather than his courageous love of truth. The reviewer for the *Westminster* found the book "very interesting," but "debatable" too. Almost all the critics viewed its author as a candidate for enrollment among the permanent British poets, and by ironic circumstance it fell to the *Sunday School Chronicle* to speculate that, if he lived and worked, Brooke might at last stand among the "great" poets of the language.[1]

As the thirty-odd reviews followed each other into print, the candidate for greatness spiralled down into what was then called a nervous breakdown. This development may be followed

---

1. A summary of reviews of *Poems,* 1911, is given in Hassall, *Brooke,* Appendix One. Others are in the Brooke Papers, King's College.

very closely through Brooke's own letters and the published letters and memoirs of friends. Separated from its chronology and details, the crack-up had five particular elements. One was vocational. Brooke in his role as man of letters had continued to move in several directions at once — as a poet, as a critic of art and thought as well as literature, and as a scholar, since he was still flogging the empty skin of his book on Webster towards the empty goal of a King's fellowship. What was he really to write? Another element was intellectual. His giddy confidence in the sufficiency of a world-view reduced to expressions about "states of mind" had disappeared, to be replaced by nagging thoughts on morality, and by an increasing knowledge that misery remains misery regardless of the mode of expression. His belief in Socialism as a value continued only as modified by awareness that it could not be a final value, and suspicion that his own dilettante efforts would not help to make it work. A third element existed in the emotional demands made on him, often unwittingly, by people he thought of as equals and friends. When properly grouped, these people had possessed a warmth and brilliance which hardly survived their taking different directions as individuals or pairs. It was now possible to find littleness, selfishness, tattling, and betrayal in the individual ex-members. Brooke's letters show that he did find these characteristics in them.

Was it possible for the ex-members to find these qualities in him? Brooke's friendship with Katherine Cox now moved into the status of a protracted sexual liaison, providing a fourth major element in Brooke's crack-up, as well as a reminder that even in his own character gilt was not gold. The affair was conducted with pretended secrecy in Italy and Germany as well as England; and Brooke's combination of self-dramatization and self-righteousness caused him to record every flutter of it in letters to friends. He even told his mother. The letters make ugly reading for their caddishness as well as their hysteria. Conversely his passion about "cleanness" and "dirtiness" crested at this time, and he studded even the most destructive of his letters to Katherine Cox with sanitary admonitions. "Oh Ka," he would write, "be clean, be clean."

These four elements of his breakdown operate against the fifth and decisive element, the protagonist of which was his mother. After the death of William Parker Brooke, Mrs. Brooke had moved off the Rugby School grounds into a house of moderate size at 24 Bilton Road, Rugby. From this place she carried on as a figure in local politics, meanwhile keeping as close to her elder surviving son as possible, and wondering what was wrong with him. Again one may follow the events, round by round and blow by blow, through the son's letters. Brooke had long since reached the conclusion that life in his mother's ambiance was impossible, and had taken to inventing the most elaborate excuses for being away from her. At the same time, he was drawn towards her by needs of his own as well as needs of hers. The relationship therefore became a series of strainings back and forth, punctuated by hints, probings, "interpretations," and judgments by two people who may after all have been very like one another.

A culmination occured in the month — the whole month — of January, 1912. Brooke was already in breakdown, vibrating wildly among responsibilities and friends, and shamefacedly trying to explain himself to a psychiatrist. In this weakness he was drawn to Cannes, on the Riviera, where he was expected to winter with his mother. Meanwhile he had arranged to winter sinfully in Germany with Katherine Cox. The letters of January, written, as Sir Geoffrey Keynes put it, "while he planned to escape his mother's vigilant eye and meet Katherine in Verona,"[2] are insane even so far as Keynes published them, and undoubtedly frantic so far as he did not. In a wild medley of deceits and revelations, plans and counterplans, "wild despair" and "awful scenes," Brooke vibrated between the two women and the various sets of values and responsibilities. When he finally broke away, leaving the Ranee "dispirited, and generous over money, and the rest," it was only to bring the same agonized confusions into the period of housekeeping with Katherine Cox, whom he wildly loved and hated, blessed and reviled, as they moved from spa to spa. He managed to torture all her petty love-secrets out of her, to leave her sick and exhausted at the end, and to parade in more mean letters his fear and concern lest she go, or go back, to other men, and become "again" involved with "uncleanness." Not discerning how neatly he had managed to punish Katherine Cox and Mary Ruth Brooke by means of one another, the friends and ex-friends to whom he explained all this "began to think he was insane." [3]

2. Keynes' note, Brooke, *Letters,* p. 331.
3. Brooke, *Letters,* pp. 333-57.

Brooke's work during this year of breakdown included good work as well as bad. His major monument in British University circles, the serio-comic place-poem "Grantchester," marked its beginning. His only play, a one-acter called *Lithuania* and set in that country, marks in several ways its middle and decisive parts. One is not really surprised to find in the hero of *Lithuania* a wanderer alone and unappreciated, and hatcheted to death by two women. After matters had become impossible, Brooke sailed for America, and the routine flatness of the journalism he sent back to England marks a sort of break with his prancing former concern over arts and ideas. If the nadir of his experience occurred in France and Germany in 1912, its clearest turning-point may have occurred in California little more than a year later, and his abso- lute recovery in England again, after another year. By that time he had taken some more serious people into his heart, opened a new poetic vein, and accepted the ruin of what had gone before.

II

The poem ultimately to be known as "The Old Vicarage, Grantchester," was written at the Cafe des Westens, a journalist's rendezvous near the Zoo Station in Berlin.[4] Brooke's first feeling towards this production was confused, so that after being called "Home" it went to "Fragments of a Poem to be entitled *The Sentimental Exile*," and finally to "The Old Vicarage, Grant- chester," a name certainly to conjure with. It is very much a Cambridge article, using all possible place-names of Cambridge, being directed immediately for publication to the journal *Basileon* of Cambridge, and being scribbled — as to the first draft — in an account book given to Brooke by Maynard Keynes, a man then mainly identified with Cambridge. Its first reader was Brooke's classmate Dudley Ward, and the various manuscripts are now to be studied in King's College.

Identifications of "The Old Vicarage" transcend the city and University, however. The poem produced and still produces reactions based on the reader's feelings towards education, tradi- tion, and nationality, as well as landscape. Trapped by their

---

4. See Hassall, *Brooke*, pp. 339-43, for an account of the composition. Hassall also, at p. 336, prints a photo of the MS.

attitudes, "new" and "social" critics discarded it. and Brooke as well, as belonging to an age which was gone and deserved to be forgotten. Trapped by other attitudes, men and women of Cambridge, and now of all British Universities, regard it as a sort of textbook, whimsical but true, on the values of past-and-present. Individual lines and couplets will be sweet or stinging to persons of special interests or special sensitivity. Brooke could not have known that in the National Socialist year of 1935 a German Ph. D., Klara Urmitzer, "1909 in Bonn geboren," would take its lines,

> England's the one land I know
> Where men of Splendid Hearts may go,

as demonstrating that "Deutsche Kultur ist für Brooke immer fremd und unverständlich geblieben."[5] Nor could he know what thoughts and images might be called up, not much later, by its merely sly little lines,

> *Temperamentvoll* German Jews
> Drink beer around.

Its power to hurt is part of its power, and in its ineffable way, through fancy, fantasy, comedy, cruelty, code-allusions, and pure sentiment, "The Old Vicarage, Grantchester," is one of the most powerful of all the world's poems on transcendental landscape.

The poem is written in the octosyllabic couplets which, since "The Fish," were becoming a familiar vernacular for Brooke. Some of the lines seem, indeed, to have been left over from that poem,

> Here I am, sweating, sick, and hot,
> And there the shadowed waters fresh
> Lean up to embrace the naked flesh.

Differences of culture then become important to the poem:

> There [at Grantchester] the dews
> Are soft beneath a morn of gold.
> Here tulips bloom as they are told;
> Unkempt about those hedges blows

5. *Rupert Brooke* (Würzburg, 1935), p. 8.

An English unofficial rose;
And there the unregulated sun
Slopes down to rest when day is done,
And wakes a vague unpunctual star,
A slippered Hesper; and there are
Meads, towards Haslingfield and Coton
Where *das Betreten*'s not *verboten.*

One finds, as expected, proper allusions to former inhabitants; a faun, a naiad, a "hundred vicars," plus curates and Rural Deans, and poets:

... the centuries blend and blur
In Grantchester, in Grantchester —
Still in the dawnlit waters cool
His ghostly Lordship swims his pool,
And tries the strokes, essays the tricks
Long learnt on Hellespont, or Styx.
Dan Chaucer hears his river still
Chatter beneath a phantom mill,
Tennyson notes, with studious eye.
How Cambridge waters hurry by.

These allusions double and triple themselves, since they allude to post-Cambridge aspects of the lives and careers of the various authors. Byron truly bathed in all those places. But Brooke does not allow the learning to clog, and soon moves into preposterous comparisons:

Cambridge people rarely smile,
Being urban, squat, and packed with guile;
And Royston men in the far South
Are black and fierce and strange of mouth;
At Over they throw oaths at one
And worse than oaths at Trumpington,
And Ditton girls are mean and dirty,
And there's none in Harston under thirty ...
But Grantchester! Ah. Grantchester!
There's peace and holy quiet there,
Great clouds along pacific skies,
And men and women with straight eyes,
Lithe children lovelier than a dream,
A bosky wood, a slumbrous stream,
And little kindly winds that creep
Round twilight corners half asleep

"Grantchester" has its flaws. Even in a spoof, a line like "children lovelier than a dream" will not do. Moreover Brooke's preoccupation with bathing and youthfulness is intrusive, and his jokes about them are heavy:

> In Grantchester their skins are white;
> They bathe by day, they bathe by night. . . .
> They love the Good, they worship Truth;
> They laugh uproariously in youth
> (And when they get to feeling old,
> They up and shoot themselves, I'm told).

That is too loose. However, it is misreading rather than exact reading which has endangered the reputation of this poem. With a certain recklessness, Brooke in the peroration allowed himself to be partly straightforward. Thus to the landscape with its intricately blended fact and fancy was added a kind of objective moral element.

> Oh is the water sweet and cool,
> Gentle and brown, above the pool?
> And laughs the immortal river still
> Under the mill, under the mill?
> Say, is there Beauty still to find?
> And Certainty? And Quiet kind?
> Deep meadows yet, for to forget
> The lies, and truths, and pain? — Oh yet
> Stands the Church clock at half past three
> And is there honey still for tea?

Read with humor, this conclusion fits other preposterous elements of the poem. But to a certain kind of unsmiling academic, it has operated as a slap in the face. Thus in her book on modern poetry, Babette Deutch coarsely referred to Brooke as a man who "wanted to drink tea in the old garden," and to the lines about the broken clock and the honey as being obsolete, the attic accumulations of an age gone by.

A working poet is responsible for making himself clear to his readers, but it is not in the creed that he must satisfy that kind of criticism. Against the charge that "Grantchester" ends too sentimentally there is not much defense. Against the charge that "Grantchester" is passé as a note on values every kind of defense is possible. By Brooke's time the cosmos ran in a circle, Shakespeare had been electronic charges, the foot of Rupert Brooke could not sink into the same river even once, let alone the twice of which the foot of Heraclitus was incapable. "All the immovable system of things I see around me, will vanish like smoke," he wrote once. "All this present overwhelming reality will be as dead and odd and fantastic as crinolones or a 'dish of tay'." Like other members of his poetical generation he was too much rather than too little aware of the transiency of a village, a vicarage, and a mood.

III

Like "The Old Vicarage," Brooke's play *Lithuania* had its inception in or near the Cafe des Westens, in Berlin. According to different accounts, he got the story from a newspaper article or from a yarn told among the newswriting patrons of the place. Unknown to him, it had formed the plot of a whole series of earlier productions – popular ballads of Wales, the Augustan play *Fatal Curiosity* by George Lillo, the Victorian play *Vae Victis* of Mrs. Oscar Berlinger, and the German melodrama *Vierundzwanzigster Februar* by Zacharias Werner. Milhaud had used the same story for his opera *Le Mâtelot*. It was a clever enough plot, but its heavily ironic twist had the defect of a base in coincidence, and Brooke knew from the outset that it would not sustain a whole evening. Encouraged by one-act successes at the Abbey Theatre and elsewhere, he wrote it as a one-acter, for playing time of about one hour. During the fall and winter of 1912 he brought it to the attention of several theatrical producers, including Granville Barker, who kept it by him for over a year but never quite decided to stage it. Stopping in Chicago on his way back from the South Seas early in 1914, Brooke read it before the dramatic circle assembled at the Chicago Little Theatre. Maurice Browne, the Englishman who headed this group, staged it successfully in October, 1915, six months after Brooke's death. Small editions of 1915 (Chicago), 1922 (Cincinnati), and 1935 (London) maintained a kind of sleepy life for the play. Only in 1970, when it was reprinted by Timothy Rogers in his collection of Brooke's work, did it become readily accessible to readers.

The well-tested plot of *Lithuania* draws its force from a conflict of too-human motivations. The son of an abjectly poor peasant couple has run away in early youth, and is thought to have died. In fact he has gone to America and made a fortune. Now he has returned with the intention of sharing his wealth with his parents. But he hesitates to announce himself, and is not recognised as the returning son. Desperate for money, his family murders him for the contents of his wallet. When that deed is done, they find out who he is, and to their natural horror of filicide is added the horror of being caught at the end. To this basic plot Brooke added some effective details of person, place, and incident. His most interesting new departure was invention of "The Daughter," a bitter, hardened, dehumanized young woman, and employment of her as chief agent in the murder. As already pointed out, the deed is shared between this woman and her mother. The pater familias, a weak and demoralized old man, has lost his nerve and is trying to recover it in a vodka stube at the time of the actual murder. As affecting the victim, this constellation may usefully be compared to the constellation in which Brooke thought himself to be fixed.

In an attractive critical essay, Maurice Browne wrote that *Lithuania* was "an *acting* play" from beginning to end. "There is no false or unnecessary word in it; the characters, the situation, the intolerable suspense, the horror of the deed, the reversal, and the appalling climax, are the work of a real dramatist."[6] These integers suggest influence of the Tudor and Stuart dramatists with whom Brooke had become so intimate. That the tightness and exactness of the play were achieved by honest effort is shown by the surviving manuscripts, where are to be found drawings of the stage, pencil sketches of the characters, and the most delicate adjustments to details of speech and stage direction. Apparently casual changes like that from "grips the table" to "looking down at the table" and "asleep against the ladder" to "asleep, collapsed at the foot of the ladder," support the characterization with precision. By these means, and in spite of their community of backgrounds and motivations, Brooke convincingly individuated each member of the family group.

Standing apart from all others is the female called The Daughter. The Daughter combines the moral degradation of Webster's bloody noblewomen, the social degradation of Zola's *lumpen* proletarians, and the flatness and automism which Brooke had found among some women of his own experience, in particular

6. *Recollections of Rupert Brooke* (Chicago, 1927), p. 52.

Miss Cox. The Daughter is not even handsome, being slightly past her youth, well past what beauty she may have had, and hopelessly past all charming or encouraging associations. Her legs are scarred and her body muscle-knotted from her work in the fields. She is ungainly and awkward in her movements, and gruntingly spasmodic in her speech. A peasant lover who has "smelled her out," as her mother puts it, produces a love connection made up of leering and lurching and ill-tempered physical wrestling. The only good qualities of The Daughter are energy and decision, and she puts these to characteristically ugly uses. When, as to the main action, her parents vacillate, she says "one must do things straight and not think." Forcing her mother to assist with the murder, she produces the most scabrous of tactical advice – "He's a weak little man. Take off your skirt and throw it over him up to the neck and hold it down so he can't get his hand out." Battering the exposed head of her brother with a crude hatchet, she keeps on "hitting and hitting" long after he is dead. Brooke permits his audience to derive a little gallows-humor giggle from the mother, who croaks over the bloody rags "I'll never use that skirt again." Nothing of the kind ever slips out of The Daughter, for whom symbols are as dead as principles. When the revelations are made, and the two parents are hysterical with horror, remorse, and fear of retribution, she only says, "they'll put me in prison." And so the play ends, taking its last note from its sordidly desensitized little heroine.

IV

As his neuroses slowly leveled out, Brooke completed his metamorphosis from a Cambridge literary figure to a national one. "The queer thing is," he reported, "that now I've hardened myself a good deal, and cut off other emotions fairly short, ambition grows in me. It's inordinate, gigantic." He added that the urge was confined to thinking "ambitious thoughts," and did not make him work, but the evidence is otherwise. During the winter of 1912-13, he published a good deal of poetry in national magazines, an effort we may follow in the next chapter. He also published criticism of a maturer kind. Though still officially a socialist and intellectual, he turned away from both politics and abstract thinking as materials for his critical writing, and devoted his attention to physical artifacts observed in their historical and social settings. Nation and place had become of importance, even in criticism. Conversely, eroticism and amativeness had become suspect. It was in this new mood that, soberly and realistically, he solidified his opinions on several poets, including Browning and Donne, and on a mixed series of dramatists, theatrical producers, and painters.[7]

Brooke's mature views on Browning, which have been discussed in their bearing on his own work, were brought to paper and published in a German magazine on the occasion of Browning's centennial. His newer views on Donne were developed in three review-articles based upon Grierson's epoch-making *Poems of John Donne,* published by the Clarendon Press, Oxford. Brooke had read the two heavy volumes with meticulous attention and given thought not only to them but to what they stood for. He thus emerged with something to say about the Clarendon, about the earlier editions of Donne's work, about the relationship of scholarship to criticism, and about Grierson's technical practice as editor, researcher, and bibliographer. In the first review, published in *The Nation* February 15, 1913, he startlingly miniaturized the history of English drama in its relation to the nondramatic work of Donne. In his observations on Donne himself, he emphasized that consolidation of opposites which he desired for his own work. Donne "saw everything through his intellect. . . . This does not mean that he felt less keenly than others; but when passion shook him and his being ached for utterance, to relieve the stress, expression came through the intellect." A product of Donne's thinking/feeling combination was his serious/humorous combination, humor being for Donne "part of his realism." Thus Donne could "combine either the light or the grave aspects of love with that lack of solemnity that does but heighten the sharpness of the seriousness." Additionally, Donne was supported by a simple colloquial language, a satiric imagination, a good education, and a full mastery of technique. In all this and more, Brooke was stiffening his own views about his own poetry, which was coming under attack from some strict Edwardians for its intellectual content and its reliance on wit and hard work.

Brooke's study of Webster and the Elizabethans continued

7. Chapter Two above. The articles cited are described in Keynes, *Bibliography of Brooke,* pp. 110-14.

to illuminate much of his thought about drama as a whole. Among his more technical articles of this period were two on Webster himself and one on modern stage design. He had, with his generation, strong curiosity about the continental dramatists headed by Ibsen; and in this period of readjustment he wrote careful reviews of the general careers of Chekhov and Strindberg, using each to establish his developing views about society. The review of Strindberg is of biographical importance. Anti-amative and anti-"feminist," it stresses Brooke's new beliefs about the sex situation in an over-developed culture:

> Strindberg . . . was a passionate lover, and he was born into an age and community tragically unfit for passionate lovers. His generation . . . in justifiable reaction against the erotic sentimentalism of their fathers, turned toward lovelessness. The morbid symptom of lovelessness is that denial of sex called feminism, with its resultant shallowness of women and degradation of man. Feminism disgusted Strindberg, who was born with a curiously high standard of emotional and intellectual morality; its accompaniments of natural and unnatural vice shocked him. We know what Shakespeare suffered through one light woman. Strindberg was plunged into a generation of light women. . . . By the standard of Strindberg's suffering and disgrace, we know our common loss.

Strindberg's distracted plunges into fantasy and irregular symbolism are seen in this review as the result of what had become, among the artistic middle classes, "the passionate enmity between men and women, the innate incompatibility." This is by contrast to Ibsen, who through his adoption of "feminism" with "cold and deliberate dirtiness" crowded the theatre with unsexed beings, "petulant hermaphrodites." Such views are usefully comparable to the views being developed in England by such writers as H. G. Wells and D. H. Lawrence. They were to be overshadowed by the military excitements of the years 1914-1915, and then to rise again as a dialectical gambit of Women's Liberation.

Chekhov also was kneaded into dialectics. Reviewing a new translation of Chekhov's plays, Brooke recognised a difference of national background which intensified the European phenomena of "modern nerves" and the struggles among "those whose bodily and instinctive selves over-ride the phantasies of their nervous imagination." The middle classes in Russia had not experienced the century of development given by destiny to the middle classes of Western Europe. Russians remain children, and so do their writers. "Chekhov is a pathetic, as Dostoyevski is a hysterical, child. . . . Chekhov's world is one of tired children, who hurt each other, but not very much, because they are not very strong." He found only a limited importance in the example of Russian writers for western ones. Lovelessness and dirtiness may be shared, indeed, but the public agonies of the Russians, including Chekhov, could not answer the expressive needs of "our more deeply emotional race." At approximately the same time Brooke composed, but left unpublished, a so-called "Ballade of Middle Age":

> The young man loves a bloody whore
> And breaks his heart to see her go. . . .
> He worships every foreign bore,
> Ibsen and Nietzsche and Rousseau
> And Dostieffsky and Tagore
> And (Oh my God) D'Annunzio:
> Each Scandinavian hurt or woe
> Whose shallowness no plummet gauged
> Is his, for all his friends to know.
> Thank God that I am middle-aged.[8]

This stiffening of nationalism is well reflected in his private letters. He had accepted, like others of his generation, the view of Germany as a model twentieth-century nation, a sort of European keystone. His loss of faith in Germany, accompanied as it was by deep psychological upsets, expressed itself in a general withdrawal of sympathy for the Continent as a whole. Undoubtedly this withdrawal of sympathy affected his literary judgments as well as his political ones.

During his bad period Brooke was able to draw upon his fairly good knowledge of painting, a knowledge he had been developing quietly, even sardonically, through his lifetime of visits to the galleries of Europe. His occasion was the celebrated exhibit of Post-Impressionist painters at the Grafton Galleries in London, in 1912. Brooke's long review, which was published in two sections, begins with an interesting generalization on the object of painting, that is "to convey the expression of an emotion of the artist, and *not* his impression of something he sees." The maxim suits the new term Expressionism which covered many of the pictures in the exhibition, though not all. Brooke's review moved

8. Brooke Papers, King's College.

into competent gallery criticism spiced with details from his own experience, such as the paintings of Kandinski in Munich and the sculpture of Eric Gill. His scepticism about the merits of the Russian post-impressionism, and also his enthusiasm for the new work of Matisse and Picasso, have been seconded by criticism since that time.

In this review Brooke did not mention his doubts as to the aesthetic potential of painting as a discipline. One short poem published by Keynes assails the whole discipline as "an evil" which "mocks the universe." In a more cheerful rejection, Brooke composed a quite charming verse parody of the Japanese water-colors which had become top vogue among fashionable people in London:

> White bloom across the sky,
> A perfect Hokasai.
>
> The blue behind the white,
> Quite delicate. Oh quite.
>
> The white against the blue,
> Artistic, through and through.

There are quite a few more stanzas of pretentious tea-party dialogue. One supposes that Brooke found Japanese art even more irrelevant to the British experience than Russian art.

V

Brooke's year-long trip to America and beyond commenced to be mooted when he was still in the deepest phase of his breakdown, and helpless to carry out the idea. Frances Cornford was the first to suggest the trip. She may have been the first, also, to accept the fact that Brooke's whole life, the whole syndrome of friends, ideas, politics, love affairs, and family relationships, had combined to ruin his peace, and to see the advantage of a clean break away from everything. Her final prescription was manual labor among lovely surroundings, specifically a job in the orange groves of Southern California. In many letters written over the months from early spring of 1913, Brooke alluded to the idea, but in a shifting way. The physical-labor part was rejected, then all parts involving labor, and finally the idea of residence in a single place. When Brooke finally took his departure, he did so as a gentleman-traveller rather than as a worker, and he never did reach Southern California or behold an orange grove. As we have seen, he was again capable of literary work; and his old connection with the *Westminster* now bore fruit by way of a contract to write articles as he moved along.

His itinerary took him first to New York, where an American lawyer practicing on Wall Street took him in hand, then north to Boston and Montreal, then westward across Canada to British Columbia, then south to San Francisco and Berkeley, where for the first time he felt happy and at home. With growing enthusiasm he entered the Pacific, staying for considerable periods in Hawaii, Samoa, Fiji, New Zealand, and especially Tahiti, which poured out all her treasures, including a native mistress, and held him steady for three months. The girl was called Taatamata and was to find a place in his poems. Returning, restless now, wanting to work, and a little debilitated by the Pacific diseases, he was in Berkeley again, then Chicago, where he stopped with Maurice Browne, and Washington, where a hopeful affair with a minor noblewoman failed to be consummated, and so back to England. It was a trip full of movement, but also full of leisure, and rich in those personal encounters which Brooke had cultivated into something like an art. The flow of letters which he sent back to England shows a steady and swift development of happiness in the surroundings and confidence in himself. His poetry budded and blossomed much as his character did. It was his beautiful year.

The articles he sent back do not express this enchantment. There where only thirteen of these, beginning with "Arrival" (in New York harbor) and concluding with "Outside" (leaving Canada, via British Columbia, for the Pacific United States). In effect this meant that the whole set was written while Brooke was still chilled, defensive, and satirically super-English, and before he arrived in the Bay cities which marked his temperamental turning-point. In addition to the "goldenness" of San Francisco, he had encountered in Berkeley, in the persons of several professors living along Piedmont Avenue, the most cultivated and yet relaxed of all the people he was to meet. In their flower-decked back yards he learned to think of Northern California as a "nation apart," "more like the English," the single American region which has "a literature and tradition of its own."[9] Much more important than these questionable views, he learned to relax, to feel appreciated, and to judge things on their merits rather than by their likeness or difference to comparable things in England.

Written before completion of this happy change, the thirteen *Westminster* articles never avoid cheekiness and provinciality. Together with two later articles, "Some Niggers" and "An Unusual Young Man," and with an idolatrous but intelligent introduction by Henry James, they were drawn into a volume in 1916, and have remained in print over the years. Through them one can learn about the rudeness of hotel clerks, the thin summer clothing of teamsters, the cheer-leader system and the electric-lighting system, and the simple-minded boastfulness of Americans and Canadians met along the way. Even when Brooke begins by praising, as when he calls Fifth Avenue "the handsomest street imaginable — what the streets of Germany try to be," or finds in the Canadian Rockies "that perfect serenity which only a perfect old age possesses," he is compulsively drawn to end in blame, so that Fifth Avenue is a "mask" concealing the horrors of Broadway, and the Rockies have no past, no legend, no "crowded presence of the dead," such as one might experience in England. The other articles are on the same order. Brooke had read Dickens and Mrs. Trollope on America, and picked up their critical mood without picking up their skill and essential fairness. Still young, uncertain, defensive, and narrow as to human experience, he was limited to the technique of comparison, and his comparisons could not involve classes of things, or general reasoning of any kind, but only a juvenile juxtaposing of one thing with one other thing — Harvard with Cambridge, Winnipeg with Grantchester, and so on. Often the result is absurd, as when he downgrades the great valleys of Banff for not being like the gorge of the St. Lawrence, thus forcing Canada to put down Canada.

Henry James stooped to blame this sort of trifling. In his introduction to the printed volume, James noticed that Brooke was gradually beginning to warm as he moved along, "for we make him out as more vivid and delightful as his opportunity grows." But James did not find the book satisfactory at any point. Brooke

---

9. Brooke, *Letters*, p. 514. The houses, but not the professors, still stand as in 1913, and the flowers still return in spring.

had struck at the easy targets, he thought, and had ignored all that was deeply important. Brooke's youth, he argued, had made Brooke too easy and forgiving, and prevented his discovery of "ultimate" truths about the Columbian land-mass. "We long to take him by the hand and show him finer lights. . . . We feel in a manner his sensibility wasted, and would fain turn it on the capture of deeper meanings." The "deeper meanings" Brooke might have recognised were of the downbeat or Ecclesiastes order. Brooke had, "in his friendly, wondering way," fallen short of "that bewildering apprehension of monotony of type, of modelling lost in the desert, which we might have expected of him, and of the question above all of what is destined to become of that more and more vanishing quantity, the American nose other than Judaic."[10] A little more of Mrs. Trollope, a touch heavier Dickens, a more philosophical unkindness, was what James wanted.

Philosophy was wanted on all sides. Brooke's own ways of being unkind were not clearly perceptible to James, whose Anglophilia of those years had not made him English, and whose ear for English shibboleths was never as good as he liked to think. Nor had the old man understood, nor did he ever understand, that Brooke undertook the long journey on account of misery, self-doubt, and the clinical fact of psychoneurosis. But when the essays were published, it was with James's essay perched in front for an introduction. Edward March added a genteel little Note in which, while it is admitted that the articles are separate, and that Brooke "would probably not have published them in their present form," they are denominated "chapters" and therefore implied to constitute a unified book. Setting aside the friendly South Seas piece called "Some Niggers," and the patriotic endpiece called "An Unusual Young Man," the articles do hang together. But they do not represent Brooke in the good moments of his travelling, or of his writing.

10. Henry James in the Preface, pp. 41-2.

Chapter Eight

EDWARDIAN, GEORGIAN, INDEPENDENT

As applied since about 1930 to groups of British poets, the terms "Edwardian" and "Georgian" convey a set of negative connotations. They suggest slight schools or turgid movements which dominate whole periods, and this suggestion runs against the grain of British poetic development. The terms themselves sprang up against the grain. The idea of an "Edwardian" poetry, this time as a movement, and a narrow and tired one at that, arose as a vehicle of rejection. Edwardians opposed Victorians. There never was a clear idea of the "Georgian" poetry, which existed only as a name, the invention of Brooke and Edward Marsh. Perhaps Georgians opposed Edwardians, but not even that was clear.

The main feature of the Edwardian quarrel with the Victorian period had been a retreat from responsibility and great aims into littleness, childishness, and concern with fruit-trees and small animals. The tone of this poetry was quiet and tired, and the discoveries it made were obvious. It went well in America under the presidency of Robert Frost, but it found no such competent administrator in Britain. Edward Thomas and Siegfried Sassoon were in it for a while. Brooke's friend Frances Cornford was a dead-center practioner, and Brooke himself, on the basis of un-characteristic poems such as "Grantchester" (read without humor) and "Oh that Apple Bloom," has been said to belong. However, if one judged him by isolated groups of poems, he could have been said to belong to any other group, and this was true of the so-called Georgians judged collectively. For the concept of Georgian was thought up and published with the single intention of drawing attention to young and energetic poets of many kinds, with many motives – a group as catholic as the Victorians, in fact. The Georgian keynotes, the only keynotes, were energy and good sense. The series of anthologies which, beginning in 1913, popular-ized, in their title, the idea of a "Georgian Poetry," was never programmatic. In the various Prefaces and Afterwords of these anthologies, Edward Marsh does not even hint at an organized thrust or a program, insisting only that the poets were new, youthful, and brightly alive.

What Robert Graves later called "the ranch-brand of the anthology" was pressed against the skins of over thirty poets. Among the leaders were such disparate figures as Walter de la Mare, John Masefield, Isaac Rosenberg, D. H. Lawrence, Sigfried Sassoon, and Edward Blunden, besides Brooke and Graves himself. Ezra Pound agreed to contribute, and would have been a Georgian poet except for a fluke of copyright. Through a set of puffing actions which Brooke began to engineer even before his departure for America, and continued through letters while abroad, the earlier numbers of 1913 and 1915 were brought to enjoy crisp sales and good reviews, and were in addition the work of good poets. Their standard could not be maintained in the later numbers, those of 1917, 1919, and 1922. The war eliminated the war poets at a great rate, taking out Brooke, Rosenberg, and Thomas permanently and Graves, Sassoon, and Blunden for the time being. Others such as D. H. Lawrence and Ezra Pound lost interest and went their own way. Missing at the very center was the wit and diplomacy of Brooke himself. Editing the later numbers alone, Marsh saw the collection of truly constructive and energetic poets disperse, and opened his pages to contributors of a different sort. The name Georgian was at last, with neat paradox, connected to exactly the relaxed, mindless, artifically primitive species of Edwardian poetry it had hoped to drive out of the field.

The progress of the term from a symbol of youth and energy to a symbol of pasture and contentment has been handsomely researched by Robert H. Ross in *The Georgian Revolt*.[1] Brooke's special connection to the term has been discussed by several writers, perhaps best by Timothy Rogers in his *Rupert Brooke*. It is interesting to speculate, as Ross and Rogers do, that the venturesome variety of Georgian Poetry as exemplified in the earlier Georgian volumes is partly an outcome of the adventurous and experimental attitude which enriched Brooke's own product. For

1. On the movements generally, see Ross, *The Georgian Revolt* (New York, 1967). Ross was the first to establish Brooke as the leading politician of the Georgians.

Brooke's range was widening. During the period in question, that is 1912 to the middle of 1914, Brooke moved on through the technical possibilities and the subjects, seldom working on one problem twice or returning to a problem once it had been solved. A certain direction may again be perceived. There was a good deal of satire, but this was personal and not offered for publication. Returning to poetry after his love smash and his neurotic smash, he wrote several witty, wry, almost shy little poems, attesting what had happened to him. As he began to center his attention on London, attending to his new friendships with real poets, actors, and other workers, and letting his unproductive Cambridge friendships slip away, the plaintive note disappears. He was already working earnestly when he commenced his travels, and he continued during the travels themselves, culminating in remarkable bursts of work during residences in Samoa and Tahiti. It would be possible to argue that "Retrospect," "Tiare Tahiti," and "The Great Lover," all written in the islands, culminate his career as a poet.

When he returned to England, it was with a sense of accomplishment as well as peace. That his belief in his own past work and his continuing potential was shared by other poets, his contemporaries, made him more useful as a diplomat and tactician of the Georgian Poetry volumes, and the attitudes for which they stand. Robert Graves wrote, "We all looked up to him as our elder brother." This was a long way to come in two years.

II

In the symbolic paradigm of men in the Western civilization, the serious and complete human being must descend into hell, suffer its torment and despair, and emerge again strengthened and informed, sometimes even beatified. Like other properties of his, Brooke's dark night of the soul had limitations. It was clearly painful but as clearly not tragic, it was intense without being deep. At the same time, it had a certain completeness and propriety, and took in all the regular steps. The first step was the step of a man in shock, and its results, familiar through the usage of other poets in shock, was an expression of blank emptiness followed by an expression of fullness through religion. Its representative poems are "In Freiburg Station" and "Mary and Gabriel."

"In Freiburg Station" need not be taken very seriously. It represents that defense against destructive items in the environment which is conducted by concentration on some simple, cheerful, irrelevant, outside item, in this case "puce gloves" worn by a passing bishop. "Mary and Gabriel," which must be taken seriously, bears the date August, 1912, and is referred to often in letters of that period. It is a complex, solemn, elaborate piece, one of Brooke's longest poems, and his only serious poem on an incident from standard Christianity. The incident is that of the Annunciation. Our Lady, still an inexperienced and shallow girl, finds Gabriel beside her, learns what her destiny is to be, feels the whole future of mankind begin to work within her body, and recognises the awesome totality of her mission.

> How should she, pitiful with mortality,
> Try the wide peace of that felicity
> With ripples of her perplexed shaken heart
> And hints of human ecstasy, human smart,
> And whispers of the lonely weight she bore,
> And how her womb within was hers no more,
> And at length hers.

Brooke's contribution included, with paradox and profundity, a great deal of painterly detail, and a persistent emphasis on the bodily and sexual aspects of the transaction by way of continued allusion to "breasts," "body," "limbs," altered respiration, "hurt or joy," and "pains to come," as well as that "womb" innocent through perpetual use among Catholics, but generally rejected, in church and out, by persons of Protestant background. The sexual reality thus becomes the determining factor in the damnation or salvation of mankind.

In making this poem, Brooke put a lot of things together. Among his sources were several painters, Italian and Pre-Raphaelite British, and several poets, including Milton and Christina Rossetti. The most curious and yet clearest source was Yeat's poem "Leda and the Swan," which dealt with the long-term results of the rape of Leda by Jupiter. Brooke's Mary is the Christian Leda. If we ask why Brooke exactly at this time, and only at this time, was drawn to the Christian story, and if we require an answer in serious harmony with Brooke's development as a man and poet, we have no alternative to the answer that he had entered the hell period and was seeking for a religious identification as means of getting out. This is a paranoid development as understood in psychiatry, and a desirable human development as understood in theology. Brooke did not go on with it, and never became either a madman or a convert to Christianity. Instead, after the time of "Mary and Gabriel," he became what, in many letters, he called "better". His biographical movements, including the adoption of London as a base, the shifts of his friendship toward more responsible and professional types, and the healing year of overseas travel, have already been described.

There was an accompanying poetical movement which divides into two distinct though somewhat overlapping parts. One of these parts had its main reference to the period of breakdown, explained as heartbreak. This part was most attractively distinguished by plaintive little poems, personal and musical, like sad songs. At its beginning it concentrated on the effects of a bad love, but later it turned to analysis, and to a discovery of causes, the main cause being found in an unsatisfactory woman. The second part of the movement found its utterance chiefly in the Pacific, and proposed calm after the storm. Its hallmarks are clarity, sobriety, and good humor, all tempered by mature experience. It keeps doing Plato. Though by no means profound, it is intellectual, and characteristically seeks its effects by division of some experimental matter into two polar opposites, one of which is to be trusted, while the other is scorned and rejected.

III

The model of the poems in which effects but not causes of heartbreak are offered is a strictly autobiographical poem called "Travel," of only eight lines:

> 'Twas when I was in Neu Strelitz
> I broke my heart in little bits.
>
> So while I sat in the Müritz train
> I glued the bits together again.
>
> But when I got to Amerhold,
> I felt the glue would never hold.
>
> And now that I'm home to Barton Hill,
> I know once broken is broken still.

The places here are all real, the German ones showing communities where Brooke and Katherine Cox spent time as lovers, and the English one a village next to, and standing for, Grantchester. In an even shorter poem, "Song: The Way of Love," Brooke reduces the whole experience to "one winter's day," and indeed to 48 syllables, the last six of which aver that "There is no more to say." In "The Way that Lovers Use," a poem Brooke sent to his more satisfactory lover Cathleen Nesbitt, but not in reference to her, he reduces the proposition that love-habits such as kissing and feeling make for health and happiness to mere wistful report, by concluding the three stanzas with, respectively, "So I have heard," "I have read as much," and "So lovers say." In "Beauty and Beauty" he offers a longer list of delightful and profitable results of love-meetings, but only as moves in the opening game, to be cancelled out in the middle game and end game, which he sadly reduces to the words "after — after" used as stanza-closers.

It will be noticed that in these song-like poems, Brooke is developing a new habit, almost a tic, of basing his poems on observed opposites, like *before/after, said/felt, ideal/real.* Using time more subtly, "Song: All Suddenly the Wind" shows a springtide (that of 1912) with the hawthornes just budding with green and a heart just budding with pain. As spring develops, "the hawthorne hedge puts forth its buds, / And my heart puts forth its pain." With more compexity, and very often in the sonnet form, he exploited the difference between views of love as between two persons, or one person split to two points of view. "Love" and "Unfortunate" use these polarities. "Love" contains, as a sort of introduction, the idea of abasement through one-sided love ("They have known shame, who love unloved"), but then presents the main argument that couples in love do not love one another, but each his own idea of the other, a familiar epistomological datum available in Plato, Browning, G. E. Moore, and many other writers known to Brooke:

> — such are but taking
> Their own poor dreams within their arms, and lying
> Each in his lonely night, each with a ghost.

The reliance on unsupported idea cannot maintain itself, and love —

> grows colder,
> Grows false and dull, that was sweet lies, at most.

Astonishment is no more in hand and shoulder,
But darkens, and dies out from kiss to kiss.
All this is love, and all love is but this.

The sonnet "Unfortunate" is distinguished by its opening lines
(quoted earlier) in which the heart "restless as a paper scrap" is
"tossed down dusty pavements by the winds." Its less distinguished main argument is a sophistication of the earlier poem
"Kindliness." A woman has accepted a lover, given him everything, healed and comforted him, and been "kinder than God,"
but really cared nothing about him. Her administrations are hateful since they arrive as impersonal charities, without that cosmic
all-absorption which, as implied in this and the cognate poems,
marks proper love. In "It's Not Going to Happen Again," a comic
poem written at Lake Louise, in Canada, Brooke takes the other
position, making his speaker realistic. Giving his lover the treat-
ment earned by representative women such as Juliet, Cleopatra,
and Helen, the realist "bundles her into the train."

In none of these poems is an evaluative line drawn between
lover and beloved. Except for allowances credited to group
differences such as that between male and female, Brooke's
skepticism, rage, and horror is drawn from the love-situation itself.
In other poems, including many written in America and the
Pacific, specific blame is meted out to the "you" whom they
address. In "Sometimes Even Now," a lively longer poem well
worth inclusion in anthologies, Brooke separates the joy of "you"
a year ago from the pain of "you" now. No longer either
"friendly" or "true," no longer offering "careless lips and flying
hair / And little things I may not tell," "you" can only be
appreciated if the speaker skips back over the year in "a prisoner's
holiday." Contorting his polar doubles into logical dilemmas,
Brooke produced a sixteenth-century-style sonnet with the exact
title, "He Wonders Whether to Praise or Blame Her," where again
he blames her. In the intellectual writhings of this poem, two
dilemmas are set up so as to produce a third dilemma, with its
conclusion. "You" is either wise or foolish, and either beautiful or
ugly; but "I" has certainly been a fool, and blind, so that "my"
former judgments are invalid, and "you" is left with (a) no valid or
meaningful praise, and (b) the valid and meaningful blame of
having been adored by a blind fool. Q.E.D. In the more
conventional sonnets "A Memory" and "Waikiki," both written in

Hawaii, Brooke is cruelly specific. The first shows a retrospective dream of a girl on a bed, offering "rest / Unhoped this side of heaven," but in a mode unacceptable because incomplete:

> It was a great wrong you did me, and for gain
> Of that poor moment's kindliness, and ease,
> And sleepy mother-comfort.

In "Waikiki," thinking back, he finds his bad old love "a tale that I have heard or known" –

> An empty tale of idleness and pain,
>   Of two that loved – or did not love – and one
> Whose perplexed heart did evil, foolishly,
> A long while since.

And in a third sonnet of the same group, "One Day," the speaker levies the blame by making the present review the past as from present innocence to past guilt,

> Just as a child, beneath the summer skies,
>   Plays hour by hour with a strange shining stone,
> For which (he knows not) towns were fired of old,
>   And love has been betrayed, and murder done,
> And great Kings turned to a little bitter mould.

Of these sonnets, "One Day" is damaged by its use of "heaven" and "God" as intensifiers, a reversion to one bad practice of Brooke's poetic boyhood, while "Waikiki" seeks to borrow force from scenic-cosmic conventions such as "the night's brown savagery" and "new stars" which "burn into the ancient skies / Over the murmerous soft Hawaiian sea," similarly a reversion. Despite routineness and minor defects, these sonnets are meaningful in the context of Brooke's development as the culmination of his love-oriented personal poems. Afterwards he wrote as a man who had been through his amative hell, and come out on the other side.

IV

The impersonal poems written from the point of view of a man whose journey through hell has ended begin with "The Funeral of Youth," a threnody of 58 mock-antique lines. The occasion was pat. Brooke was staying in Cornwall with the Cornfords, but not taking part in any of their comings and goings, and not interested in Frances Cornford's plan that he heal his soul by bodily labor. Lying on the floor, he wrote not only the poem but a letter to Edward Marsh, asking to be taken into Marsh's flat in London for the winter.[2] In one symbolic swoop, as we may think, he wrote himself out of his old life, and into the mature but death-oriented life which he was to lead from that point on.

Threnodies are laments for the dead. Brooke's threnody takes the form of a spoof, but it is of interest and has been anthologized repeatedly. Its format and style imitate those moving pageants composed of personified abstraction which had endured as serious poetry from Spenser's time to that of Pope's *Dunciad*, after which it became a comedy form. The abstractions which are made human and collected at Brooke's funeral include Folly, Laughter, Romance, Innocence, Ignorance, and Friendship, each of which is given a characteristic suitable to its place in Brooke's personal system. His poetical skills, "Colour, Tune, and Rhyme," attend together "as fatherless children . . . uncomprehending." Bearing new flowers, Spring came, "but did not stay for long."

> And Truth, and Grace, and all the merry crew
> The laughing Winds and Rivers, and lithe Hours;
> And Hope, the dewy-eyed; and sorrowing Song; —
> Yes, with much woe and mourning general,
> At dead Youth's funeral.

The cause of Youth's death is not stated till the end, when it is specified that Love did not attend, having died earlier, and, by inference, having by death brought about the death of the Youth.

Youth out of the way, and Love having been given her thorough post-mortem in the poems just considered, Brooke was ready to establish his role as a senior philosopher tilting graveward. His earliest poems under this identity include several deliberate reminiscences raised from personal to general status by their quick shifts of attention from love to life, and life seen in terms of regulation and law. His typical crux contrasts time as it is experienced in the physical world with time as it might be conceived in the fixed, frozen, unchanging world associated with Plato's philosophy. Brooke presented this crux first in "The True Beatitude," a poem dated as from London just before he sailed for America. In "The True Beatitude" he reintroduces his boyhood

2. Hassall, *Brooke*, pp. 273.

conception of an ugly God and a vicious Heaven. In the crux, however, eternity is made the main property of Heaven, and the love of "we" is made important exactly because of its failure to involve eternity. Given its imputed ugliness and viciousness, eternity would dirty "our" love, while temporality would save it —

> Still temporal, still atmospheric,
> Teleologically unperturbed,
> Untrodden of God, by no Eternal curbed.

In this poem the values come from two vulgarly jangling sources, abstract philosophy and personal antichristianity, with vulgarly certain results. Less contorted by hatred of a suburban John Rump divinity is "Mutability," another sonnet, this time begun in London and completed at Makaweli, in Hawaii. "Mutability" has only the Platonic abstractions:

> They say there's a high windless world and strange
> Out of the wash of days and temporal tide,
> Where Faith and Good, Wisdom and Truth abide,
> *Aeterna corpora,* subject to no change.

If what "they say" is true, "imperishable Love" is also to be found. But our experience, says the sayer, shows nothing like this. People are "straws" on "the dark flood" who "cling, and are born into the night apart." It will be noted that the terrestriality and temporality of love gladly praised by Brooke in "The True Beatitude" is sadly lamented in "Mutability." The crux is constant, but he is on one side and then the other. He liked to work with a thought, but was never very firm on what he thought about the thought.

Going on with the thought, and again forcing his opening by asserting a "they" and a "they say," he wrote "The Clouds" while at sea. In "The Clouds," a sonnet, he builds an octet which likens the great South Pacific cloud-masses to groups of quiet, profound, sympathetic personalities, and a sestet which observes that "if the dead die not" (as "they say") they might well live on as cloud-clusters of the great ocean.

> I think they ride the calm mid-heaven as these,
> In wise majestic melancholy train,
> And watch the moon, and the still-raging seas,
> And men, coming and going on the earth.

The flaw here would be in the single word "raging," which breaks crudely into the serene thoughtfulness of this good sonnet. If a companion poem entitled "Sonnet: Suggested by Some of the Proceedings of the Society for Psychical Research" is taken seriously at all, a more seismic flaw reveals itself. Dead people specifically lovers reappear here. Brooke argues that a still-loving couple, eternally happy, "beyond the sun," will refuse to move back to a dark parlor at the bidding of a spiritualistic medium, a concept evident without argument. On this forensic nothing Brooke squanders some of the loveliest imagery in this group of speculative poems:

> . . . turn and run
> Down some close-covered by-way of the air,
> Some low sweet alley between wind and wind,
> Stoop under faint gleams, thread the shadows, find,
> Some whispering, ghost-forgotten nook, and there,
> Spend in pure converse our eternal day.

The poem ends in another conceit, by which the body and senses are seen, still Platonically, to inhibit rather than promote experience. Knowledge is prevented by "this tumultous body." Without body, knowledge is at last possible. Thus we "feel, who have laid our groping hands away," and "see, no longer blinded by our eyes." This principle was to return more than once in Brooke's short remaining career, and was to help him out of it as a feature in the swan-song sonnets *1914*.

V

The five or six sun-bathed poems which Brooke wrote in and around Tahiti in the winter and early spring of 1914 make up the best of his bunched efforts. In these poems, looked at collectively, he showed not only ease and skill but a tranquil certainty and power never his before. What he thought of the jumbled "Great Lover" is uncertain, but he correctly believed that in "Tiare Tahiti" he had made octosyllabic verse his own property; and he had equal confidence that his sonnets of the long voyage would stand up against anybody's sonnets. Technically yes; but intellectually he was going backward. Placing his whole dependence on points he felt able to make, jeeringly, against his bit of philosophy and bit of religion, he was skipping right past Germany and Cambridge and arriving in Rugby again. Meanwhile his ambitions had blurred, so that while continuing to think of himself as a man of letters he had stopped projecting himself as a poet. And of great importance is the fact that during the voyage, and then in Tahiti, he was writing himself out of the world. Hardly less than in the sonnets *1914,* written a year later, he was speaking back from completion, as to the living from the dead.

The most interesting of his last group, from the standpoint of technical mastery, are "Fafaia" and "Retrospect." Both poems are in octosyllabic couplets. "Fafaia" has specific grouping of lines and movement which belongs to the Shakespearean sonnet, and, as though that idea would overbalance error, such doubtful items as a country-style "year" meaning "years" and such uncomfortable rhyme-groups as *Year/dear/years/hears* and *bright/night/white/ night.* The neat governing paradox is just that which Brooke had used in 1908 for "The Jolly Company," namely the closeness and fondness of stars to one another as observed from the earth, and their distance and alienation from each other as observed from their own positions. Brooke humanized this point by the rhetorical device of saying it lectorially to an ignorant girl, Fafaia, and by focussing from heaven to humanity at the end:

> Heart to heart is all as far
> Fafaia, as star to star.

"Retrospect" is the last and best of the poems in which Brooke saluted the greater warmth, serenity, and animal strength supposed to be found in women as over men. Katherine Cox has been said to be the original, but the lines would probably fit Taatamata, Brooke's Tahitian lover, just as well. The speaker mourns the loss of the woman's "still delight / Quiet as a street at night"; he yearns to come back to her "silence without wind or tide"; he is desolated through loss of that "infinite deep − a pool unstirred" which is her character. As though accepting a challenge, Brooke used extreme terms:

> In your stupidity I found
> The sweet hush after a sweet sound . . . .
> And when you thought, it seemed to me
> Infinitely, and like the sea,
> About the slight world you had known
> Your vast unconsciousness was thrown.

Brooke's old anguish over the absence of mad passion in a woman's love is given the sweetest expression he was ever able to give it:

> Love, in you, went passing by
> Penetrative, remote and rare,
> Like the bird in the wide air,
> And, as the bird, it left no trace
> In the heaven of your face.

"Heaven" (here as a joke) and "Tiare Tahiti" pursue the dipole of otherwhere/here, or eternity/now, "Heaven" working through religion and "Tiare Tahiti" through philosophy, both by the mode of contempt. "Heaven" stars a fish permitted to ponder with "deep wisdom" that narrow jumble which Brooke took to be the Christian religion. It is a swift poem, amusing in its compilation of pro-God phrases from *In Memoriam,* Aristotle, and selected books of the Bible:

> More than mundane weeds are there,
> And mud, celestially fair;
> Fat caterpillars drift around
> And paradisal grubs are found;
> Unfading moths, immortal flies,
> And the worm that never dies.

God himself is a water-creature. In the much richer poem "Tiare Tahiti," a philosophical rather than a religious eternity is offered. This poem completes Brooke's long series of speculations about the Ideas of Plato's universe, and is both accurate and amusing in its pairings of observed lower-world items with corresponding Ideal items:

> Songs in Song shall disappear;
> Instead of lovers, Love shall be . . .
> And my laughter, and my pain,
> Shall home to the Eternal Brain.
> And all lovely things, they say,
> Meet in Loveliness again.

Brooke's language often slips. Like the pairs above, *"feet"* go amusingly to *"Ambulation,"* and *"mouths"* to *"Mouth"*; but it is sloppy to add *"moons"* going to *"Day"* and *"hearts"* going to *"Immutability,"* pairs based on a different principle; while to say unpairingly that on "On the Ideal Reef / Thunders the Everlasting Sea" confuses doubly, spoiling the frozen stillness of the Ideal by belonging indifferently to common literary language and to the special mock-philosophic language of this poem. Brooke could not handle precise discriminations any more. "Tiare Tahiti" does not abide our question, however. Its octosyllables move gracefully enough through the merely negative-philosophic part, dance their way into a second part in which the philosophic conceit is combined with the fleshly South Seas data of warmth and sweet human beings and untroubled love, and rise to one of the most entrancing verse-paragraphs ever written about happy hours of two lovers side by side, and all "this side of Paradise." Isolated at the end of "Tiare Tahiti" is a sentence taken from a couplet of Pope's: "It is folly to be wise." Wisdom here is taken to mean philosophic or religious consideration of a sort which would prevent immediate pleasure, specifically pleasures of physical things, the senses, and the flesh.

Lumbering into view as the closing poem of the South Seas group, and also the closing poem of Brooke's pre-war poetic development, is "The Great Lover." "The Great Lover" is a strangely irregular poem, comically over-written at beginning and end, and carelessly, or defiantly, underwritten in the middle. Its bombast and portentousness echo those of Brooke's Rugby and Cambridge juvenilia. Particular threads connect it to "Dedication" (1904) and "My Song" (1907), both of which propose to perpetuate love through their own continued existence as poems. In "The Busy Heart," a good sonnet of 1913, Brooke had edged closer by placing total reliance on a list of physical things and events comforting to a lovelorn speaker who "dares not go empty-hearted." Even earlier he had fallen into the twitching habit of writing down long and often repetitive lists of pleasant things and experiences in his letters, and the best earlier cognates are to be found among these.[3] As we have seen, he had also fallen into a compulsion to write crux-poems which explore the relations of the ideal and eternal to the wordly and passing, sometimes following into the ideal, but more often mocking and rejecting it, as he did in the just-completed "Heaven" and "Tiare Tahiti." In the lumpy context of "The Great Lover" he goes both ways, saving his own soul alive and happy, but preserving also the ecstatic essences of passing experience.

The poem opens reasonably, but soon develops such ragfair

3. Brooke, *Letters*, e.g. at pp. 320, 345, 375, 503-04, 518.

grandeurs as a night (the poet's life) "remembered for a star / That outshone all the suns of all men's days," and a darkness in which appears "the inenarrable godhead of delight."

> Love is a flame: — we have beaconed the world's night.
> A city: — and we have built it, these and I
> An emperor: — we have taught the world to die.
> So, for their sakes I loved, ere I go hence,
> And the high cause of Love's magnificence,
> And to keep loyalties young, I'll write those names
> Golden for ever, eagles, crying flames,
> And set them as a banner, that men may know,
> To dare the generations, burn and blow
> Out on the wind of Time.

Brooke's hyperboles seem to proceed from the more hyperbolic of Shakespeare's love sonnets. But his "lovers" so gorgeously announced turn out to be china plates, crusts of bread, "holes in the ground," sheets and blankets, and a train, as well as the standard sophist-rustic-Edwardian oak trees, horse chestnuts, campfire smoke, and "footprints in the dew." Technical no-no's such as epithets, pathetic fallacies, and false rhyme, are regally tossed in. In the third part of the poem, sharply distinct though visually enjambed, he returns to the lurid sky-writing of the first part:

> And these shall pass
> Whatever passes not, in the great hour,
> Nor all my passion, all my prayers, have power
> To hold them with me through the gate of Death.
> They'll play deserter, turn with the traitor breath,
> Break the high bond we made, and sell Love's trust
> And sacramented covenant to the dust.

And so to the paraxodical, or merely confused, philosophic conclusion. There Brooke avers that after death he will awaken, and be eternal, but not cleansed or perfected since to "new friends, now strangers," he will be able to give only "what's left of love." In his boyish early poetry he had imagined himself blasted, looking back from hell, and he had never really left the concept. Meanwhile the beloved objects "The Great Lover" has left behind will be enjoyed by others, but not for long, since their destiny is to "change," "break," "grow old," "blow about," fade out and die, till, as a two-word sentence dramatically set off as an independent line assures us, "Nothing remains." The gnarly final couplet gives the rest:

> O dear my loves, O faithless, once again
> This one last gift I give: that after men
> Shall know, and later lovers, far-removed,
> Praise you, 'All these were Lovely'; say, 'He loved.'

There is a force and power in "The Great Lover" which Brooke seldom touched elsewhere. Brooke printed it in *New Numbers* when he returned to England, and it apparently got by without comment. When the *1914* sonnets and his own death had made him famous, it became famous too, as representing the poetic testament in which the dead poet had reviewed his whole experiential life. Later it attracted some thought in youth circles, and was reprinted in college anthologies in America. It is a kind of microscopic *Moby Dick* or *King Lear*, where in spite of every possible lapse and fallacy a memorable impression manages to be made.

Chapter Nine

NINETEEN FOURTEEN

Brooke's aversions had diminished during his sojourn in the tolerant South Seas, and he reentered America in a more generous spirit. His Berkeley friends took him in again, and he proceeded eastward as from friend to friend, stopping in Chicago, Pittsburgh, New York, and Washington, where the particular friend was the Marchesa Capponi. He was beginning to think of work again. Poetry, or serious writing of some kind, was occasionally mentioned in the letters, but was obviously not of much interest to him. Now that he had broken into overseas journalism, he thought of going on with that. Passing through the Southwest, with a three-day pause at the Grand Canyon, he heard a good deal about the Mexican revolution, fancied that Pancho Villa's soldiery might come "up from El Paso," and thought of going into Mexico himself as a war correspondent. In letters of the year before he had whimpered about going to the Balkans as a correspondent "if Russia and the rest of them fight," and had expressed the thought that his death by "a stray bullet or the cholera" might be "the best solution all around." Now he drew back from the experience of blood in Mexico under the mistaken idea that "it won't be much of a war," and said nothing about his own need to die.

With equal cheerfulness and lack of knowledge he laid down a series of pronouncements on economics, Socialism, strikes, women, the militant groups in American labor, and the possibility of returning to the South Seas as a conquerer in a "2000-ton yacht" which he urged a millionaire friend to buy. His letters continued to vary according to the particular recipient, so that he talked socialism to one friend, intellectualism to another, and "feminism" to a third, usually playing up to the addressee and never giving offense, but never being lovable either.[1] He went on with his one American flirtation. The Marchesa Capponi was an

1. Brooke, *Letters*, p. 583.

American woman, well travelled, sophisticated, and still developing herself by the study of education with Madame Montessori, in Washington. She was so frank as to have called on Mrs. Brooke in Rugby while Brooke was in Tahiti, an act which pleased Mrs. Brooke but took her son aback. As he moved over the curving surface of the United States, Brooke repeatedly hinted that she should take him into her house on R Street, in the capital.

> I shall reach Washington dishevelled, dirty, tired and bad-tempered, and in rags . . . .
>
> I shall require you to tell me what to buy and where to buy it and how much to eat, and when to go to bed, and where to stay, and what to see, and what to say, and when to brush my hair and wash my hands. Will you?
>
> It will be heavenly, seeing you . . . .
>
> Don't be too busy when I'm in Washington – have you a house there? I want to lie on a sofa and talk. There's lots of things I want.[2]

The Marchesa was not Bohemian and not spaciously set up, and he stayed at the Willard Hotel instead of her house.

Meanwhile, as his trains moved into Middle America, he went back to slandering the host nation. His term for Americans he approved of was "most un-American," and he wrote jingles about "Plutocracy," an evil concept he thought of as peculiarly American. The single correct country turned out to be England. In a letter to Frances Cornford, he spoke about the swelling up of his "English thoughts." Later he would need to face some bad English facts – "when everything's *too* gray, and there's an amber fog that bites your throat, and everyone's irritable and in a high state of nerves, and the pavement's too greasy, and London is full of 'Miles of shopping women, served by men,' and another Jew has bought a peerage, and I've a cold in my nose, and the ways are full of lean and vicious people, dirty, hermaphrodites and eunuchs, Stracheys, moral vagabonds, pitiable scum." Eventually England would be as terrible as America, he said; and he specified a set of oncoming American terrors, the results of America's being "ruled by women," and concluded with his familiar diatribe against "feminism" and for feminity. But now his English thoughts were "grey, quiet, misty, rather mad, slightly moral, shy, and lovely thoughts"[3]

2. Brooke, *Letters,* pp. 575-90, passim.
3. Brooke, *Letters,* p. 573.

He sent in more of these specifications from New Mexico, Chicago, and New York, concluding with a great whoop of joy addressed to Cathleen Nesbitt from Washington:

> — I sail from New York on May 29: and reach Plymouth (o blessed name o loveliness! Plymouth — was there ever so sweet and droll a sound? Drake's Plymouth! English, western Plymouth! city where men speak softly and things are sold for shillings, not for dollars, and there is love and beauty and old houses, and beyond which are little fields, very green, bounded by small piled walls of stone — and behind them — I know it, the brown and black, splintered, haunted moor. By that the train I shall go up — by Darmouth, where my brother was — I will make a Litany — by Torquay, where Verrall stayed, and by Paignton, where I have walked in the rain: past Ilsham, where John Ford was born, and Appledore, in the inn of which I wrote a poem against a Commercial Traveler; by Dawlish, of which John Keats sang; within sight of Widdicomb, where old Uncle Tom Cobbley rode a mare; not a dozen miles from Galsworthy at Manaton; within sight, almost, of that hill by Drewsteignton on which I lay out all one September night, crying. And to Exeter. And to Ottery St. Mary, where Coleridge sojourned; And across Wiltshire, where men built and sang many centuries before the aquila . . . Oh, noble train, oh glorious and forthright and English train, I will look round me at the English faces and out at the English fields — and I will pray . . .) — reach Plymouth, as I was saying when I interrupted, on Friday June 5.

The list, or litany, is worth inspection. It presents under analysis five separate units of experience — Landscape, Tradition, Literature, Friends, and Self, with the last unit expressed as a set of significant emotional responses. Politics, economics, social welfare, general education, and every sort of personal aspiration or activity are left out. These "English thoughts" are not even free-standing, their combination of sentiment and soft amusement having become current among the reading population in the first timid reaction to the clear evaluationism and social awareness of the Victorians. Nor did Brooke himself take them seriously, at the time. Distilled into the *1914* sonnets as "thoughts by England given," they were to capture the nation only a little while later.

II

Brooke's train passed from Plymouth through the designated country items, and arrived safely in Victoria Station on

June 5. Edward Marsh was waiting on the platform and there was great deal to discuss. Thanks to Marsh's work as agent and publicist, Brooke's reputation had improved during Brooke's absence. It was not yet a national reputation. But it ran through some powerful divisions of the population, and could become national with a little pushing. Marsh was for a consolidation of the reputation, and for readying for the next and final push. In Marsh's loving view, Brooke was already a finished poet, and was destined for the position that Tennyson and Arnold had occupied the century before.

Looking about again, Brooke found himself a cherished member of three separate though overlapping circles. One was composed of his original friends, men and women who had become connected with him through their connection to the public-schools and universities, with Cambridge friends still naturally in the lead. Frances Cornford, Jaques Raverat, and Geoffrey Keynes were the most important people here, while Noel Olivier and Katherine Cox provided the romantic excitement, and about a dozen other names completed the list. The second circle was made up of people actually working in the arts, and especially in poetry. The serious younger poets John Masefield, John Drinkwater, Walter de la Mare, and Lascelles Abercrombie loomed most importantly in this group, at least from Brooke's point of view. Cathleen Nesbitt had her all-important place there, and exotics like Katherine Mansfield, Isaac Rosenberg, and Ezra Pound moved in the gypsy half-light beyond the edge of the circle. Many self-standing writers such as Henry James and D. H. Lawrence maintained contact with Brooke in his role as a member of this group. Visual artists appeared in it and disappeared. The Bloomsbury group had now found its members, and so had the corresponding circle pulled together by Lady Ottoline Morrell; but Brooke's only contacts were through Virginia Woolf and D. H. Lawrence, and even these contacts attenuated as Bloomsbury and the Morrell clique moved towards pacifism and internationalism, while Brooke turned soldier and patriot. The leading members, genuine inventors like Bertrand Russell and Maynard Keynes, had never taken Brooke seriously, and he had lumped them all with Lytton Strachey as intellectual parasites and moral degenerates. They too found their place in the *1914* sonnets.[4]

4. Especially in "Peace," as "half-men, with their dirty songs and dreary."

The third circle to which Brooke now had entry was the power circle. It was headed by Anthony Asquith, the Prime Minister, Winston Churchill, then the First Sea Lord and an in-and-out cabinet minister, and other men and women who had brought their aristocratic names into the politics of the House of Commons. Their bases, which now became the frequent bases of Brooke, were town mansions and country estates, and home base for them all was 10 Downing Street, where Brooke moved about freely. The females of special interest here were Violet Asquith, to whom Brooke wrote many letters from America and the Pacific, and Lady Eileen Wellesley, daughter of the Duke of Wellington, a pretty and intelligent girl with whom Brooke formed a quite serious relationship. Lady Eileen's letters were among the two groups which he instructed to be burned, when, in the Mediterranean, he was preparing for his death. Of the younger men in this circle Arthur Asquith, called Oc, was Brooke's particular friend. Unlike Bloomsbury and the friends of Lady Ottoline, Brooke's Downing Street friends took Brooke seriously as a poet, and even as a thinker, and tried to protect him. Noticing his frequent sickness in the training period, many of them advised him to abandon his commission for reasons of health. Their long arm followed him to Egypt, where he lay prostrate with sunstroke and camp dysentary, and offered him a non-combat appointment on the staff of Sir Ian Hamilton, the commanding general of the expedition and himself a member of the Downing Street circle. Their arm followed Brooke even to Skyros, and solicitous radio messages from the Admiralty and 10 Downing Street were crackling about him as he died.

Sponsorship of Brooke in the circle of creative spirits, and a little later in the circle of power, was the work of Edward Marsh. Marsh's programs were usually based on the principle of bringing together people who had mutual interests and corresponding needs. Following this principle, he played down Brooke's old Cambridge friendships, brought him into contact with the serious poets and artists of the day, and provided some romance through the introduction of Cathleen Nesbitt. As a gentleman-secretary, well equipped with social poise and diplomatic presence, Marsh was on Winston-and-Clemmie terms with the Churchills, as well as being trusted by other politicians for his tact and by their hostessing wives for his social skills. When Brooke was ready,

Marsh easily extended his aquaintance into this group. His influence was important even after August, 1914. Through it, Brooke got his commission in the Naval Reserve and his appointment to the Royal Naval Division, and later benefitted by a manipulation of assignments designed to bring together a sort of sub-lieutenant elite through which Brooke and Arthur Asquith were surrounded with familiar and agreeable fellow-officers. Marsh's helpfulness, projected through the Prime Minister and the First Sea Lord, and lasting to the grave and beyond it, was the essential factor in Brooke's quick beatification as a national poet and national martyr.

Brooke's successes in the months between his arrival home and his enrollment as a marine officer were on the Marsh system, being more concerned with sales promotion and literary politics than with creative work. Neglecting Grantchester and Rugby, and using Marsh's London flat as a base, he made a glittering re-entry into the offices and cafes where literature seemed to be made. Following Marsh, he attached himself to the activities of the *Poetry Review* and Poetry Bookshop, two apparently sound institutions controlled by Harold Monro. On the basis of his earlier work, plus the influence of Marsh and other friends, he came to be regarded as a coming man by Monro and his associates. The volumes to be called *Georgian Poetry*, originally the result of an exchange between Brooke and Marsh, advanced in harmony with the interests of the Bookshop and the *Review*, and Brooke astonished some friends "from the spectacular point of view" by producing poems merely "because Monro wanted them." The advertising campaign for *Georgian Poetry* was the work of Brooke and Marsh together. While in Canada Brooke had been promoted into a little collection of poets – Gibson, Abercrombie, Drinkwater, and himself – who hoped to go forward as a group. Brooke was happily surprised, finding the conjunction "rather a score for me, as my public is smaller than any of theirs."[5] Once more the manipulator had been Marsh. The new group enterprise, a periodical called *New Numbers,* was Brooke's principal outlet during 1913 and 1914. In its third number he reprinted the South Seas poems and in the fourth his war sonnets. Among his other benefactions, Marsh caused a copy of *New Numbers* to be

5. Ross, *The Georgian Revolt,* pp. 97ff.

flourished on the stage during performance of a popular play. Unlike almost all such publications, *New Numbers* paid for itself from the first, with some profits left over for division among the four poets.

It is hard to find a parallel for Brooke's feat of expanding his relationship three-fold, and among the three essential parts of the society, in so short a time, and with so little productive effort. No serious work appeared; there is no poetry, and almost no prose, in all the months between the South Seas poems and August, 1914. Some of his contemporaries, including Virginia Woolf and Frances Cornford, came to believe that he was dropping out of literature and would enter politics, not the air-spun intellectual politics of the Cambridge years, but the hard-fisted parliamentary sort whose masters he now found himself dining with. Such a career would have been possible enough. Being personal rather than professional, his growing popularity was suitable for conversion to the uses of almost any calling. And his Cambridge fancies, including Socialism, abstract philosophy, and the cult of youth, had faded almost white.

III

Hassall and Keynes, as well as less significant commentators, have averred that Brooke's idealistic enthusiasm about the war, and indeed his whole system of self-sacrificial patriotism, would not have survived a closer view of the ugliness and butchery which modern wars visit upon their participants.[6] Important arguments exist on the other side. Though Brooke might have joined the reportorial "war poets" after their fearful images of blood and dirt had become modish, he was too thoroughly committed to general idealism, the romantic view, and the Government position, to make an exception in the single area of war. The "war poets" belong to naturalism and rebellion; Brooke never really did. Again, though death is almost always undesirable. Brooke's verse had been handling it with exultation from the very beginning. As we have seen, Platonic questions had taken command of his thinking, and had so captured him that he was able to claim, even in private

6. Hassall, *Brooke*, p. 531; Keynes, notes in Brooke, *Letters*, p. xiii and p. 558.

letters, that "Death is not important." The 1914 sonnets confirm this cut-rate view of death. Thirdly, the war simplified and smoothed all aspects of his own life. In a practical way, it solved his career problems, family problems, love problems. More than that, it gave his previously confused desires a single theme and goal, one central object around which he could group all the rest, and an object which was pleasingly shared by most of the nation. As though by magic he had moved his Hamlet-like doubts and indecisions through four acts, and become like Hamlet in the fifth act, past all complexities, a deliberate unity, a single thing.

His being programmed to consider the ideals of the war and ignore its consequence was strongly supported by his new associations. The clique now at the top of his system was the government clique and the voices he heard were government voices. His own voice was soon among them. Belgium was the cry of the day, and his letters droop under the weight of his earnestness on that key item of war thinking. Similarly he worked at Culture versus *Kultur* and democracy versus military oligarchy, and explained, especially in letters to America, how helpful an American intervention might ultimately be. Many of his intellectual and artistic friends were developing attitudes and positions rather than enlisting; and he addressed admonitory arguments to some, while quietly dropping away from others. Soon "weak as a Pacifist" became a regular term of invidious comparison. Twice he began regular articles in support of enlistments. One, written on the letterhead of his battalion, describes the confusion of an invented pacifist, "Theodore Ripe." Brooke declares his neutrality toward Ripe; he is "only to relate," not to judge. However, the heavy language of his approach shows his intention of exposing egotism and fallacy in Ripe's pacifist convictions. The other essay, perhaps more important, is about a man who "feared shadows." The man "strangely" did not fear darkness, but only mixed lights, dappling, chiaroscura. The simplicity of service in right-and-wrong, pure-and-dirty situations, such as a just war, would have cleared away this man's confusions and made him a happier man.[7]

Brooke's presentation of the theme of sacrifice found its main place in an article called "An Unusual Young Man," written

7. The Brooke Papers, King's College, engross both essays.

in early August, 1914, and published in *The New Statesman*. Though some data are changed and third-person grammar is used, Brooke himself is the young man. He is pictured on a beach in Cornwall when news arrives that the war has begun; and he climbs to a bluff and looks out over the water, contemplating the meaning of the news to him. His thoughts are allowed to drift by free association, but their movements soon divide into two clear parts, "the upper running about aimlessly from one half-relevant thought to another, the lower unconscious half laboring with some profound and unknowable change." Concerns of the upper division are partly practical – here are questions about how his career, his entertainments, and his life generally will be altered by the war. Included are recollections of Germany in its most pleasant aspects, the Starnberger Sea at evening, a woman singing as she hangs clothes on a line, and a night of poetic drunkenness with young Germans in a student kneipe in Munich. But the young man's deeper self, what he called the "lower unconscious," meanwhile stirs and moves. His mother and his lover, "someone called A———," exist on this level, and something else "was growing in his heart, and he couldn't tell what." It was very obscure. The ocean waited. "But as he thought *England and Germany,* the word *England* seemed to flash like a line of foam."

> With a sudden tightening of his heart, he realized that there might be a raid on the English coast. He didn't imagine any possibility of its *succeeding,* but only of enemies and warfare on English soil. The idea sickened him. He was immensely surprised to perceive that the actual earth of England held for him a quality which he found in A———, and in a friend's honour, and scarcely anywhere else, a quality which, if he'd ever been sentimental enough to use the word, he'd have called "holiness." His astonishment grew as the full flood of "England" swept him on from thought to thought. He felt the triumphant helplessness of a lover.

Brooke went on to list the familiar units of landscape and population – flowers, fields, "the Cotswolds, and the Weald, and the high land in Wiltshire," with a "multitude of faces," and, most earnestly, his mother and lover again. "To his great disgust, the most commonplace sentiments found utterance in him. At the same time he was extraordinarily happy." This manner of tracing country-love to the same deep impulses which produce mother-love and sexual love became the psychoanalytic justification for his other wartime utterances, including the *1914* sonnets. Any such experience of love bursting from the unconscious becomes the focusing element of all the affections. The commonplace expression "and I would die for you" arises naturally in such transactions.

Such a focusing will also simplify the life before the death. As he explained to friends, his sufficient function while in uniform was "to kill Germans," and all the bother of mud and training and military regulations was worthwhile as supporting the function. Contents, attitude, and style of the military notebooks he left behind him stand to corroborate. In these notebooks, for the first time since his school days, he maintained objectivity and clarity in the face of all temptations towards ornamental ironies, and wrote like Defoe or Bunyan, or any common soldier.

> German method of advance: a front of cavalry, in close contact with Jagers and machine guns in big lorries. When our cavalry engage them, they fall back and expose infantry (deployed). They always combine MG with entanglements: leaving gaps on purpose.
> They put MG's in houses and let our men pass then fire.

Some of the instructions seems especially shaped for the use of a platoon leader pushing soldiers under the conditions expected at Gallipoli:

> Fire is cover.
> Make them understand, *they must get on.*
> Push on – Infantry.
> Obstacles v. important. Make them out of something, somehow.
> Pits with stakes, as at Antwerp.

The common rifle, lord of battles so long as a front could move, received a homage based on genuine admiration:

> MG not so imp. as rifle
> 3 forces acting on bullet: explosion of cartridge, resistance of air, and force of gravity. Rifle originally sighted with regard to resultant of all three.
> Pull through:/ (1) from breach/ (2) continuous pull/ (3) cord must not wear on barrel./// Chief faults: / (1) cordworn barrel/ (2) gauze used every day / (3) pulling from muzzle – gets cordworn chamber and blows your eye out.[8]

8. Military notebooks in the Brooke Papers.

Even on the transport *Grantully Castle,* between sicknesses and "weak as a pacifist," he was busy with the simple lore and simple language. "Clearing jams," he jotted. "Biff up. Down sight. Up. Cover. Clear lock. Load." The unsmiling earnestness of these notes speaks for Brooke's view, expressed as a concept elsewhere, that he was getting himself free of doubt and vanity, and operating as a whole man.

IV

Brooke wrote one war sonnet entitled "The Treasure" in August, 1914, while seeking his military opportunities, and the five others collectively entitled *1914,* numbered I to V, and also titled "Peace," "Safety," "The Dead (I)," "The Dead (II)," and "The Soldier," as a single effort at the end of the year, while serving as a sub-lieutenant. There are consequently either five or six sonnets in *1914,* depending on the point of view. Though writing the five cognate sonnets more or less to order (for *New Numbers*), Brooke had let them take their own forms in a process he compared to "developing photographs," and was pleased when he found one "turning out fairly good." All of them are about death as sacrifice. Their genesis and development has been discussed by stage in several biographies. Though nowadays more abused than praised, they were important national poetry in their own calamitous day. As Brooke's last finished work, and the work by which he was best known in his life, they deserve careful reading.

The rhetorical approach of these sonnets differs in the fact that the sacrificial dead persons are *"we"* in "Peace" and "Safety," *"they"* in "The Dead (I)" and "The Dead (II)," and *"I"* in "The Soldier" and "The Treasure." They also differ in the mode of address, "Peace," "The Dead (II)," "The Soldier," and "The Treasure" existing as open lyrics, addressed to any hearer, while in "Safety" a loved person is addressed. All six have a disciplined separation between octet and sestet, neither grammar nor sense carrying over. "The Treasure" is octosyllabic and has its octet and sestet turned upside down, but all the rest are standard decasyllabic sonnets. Except for "The Dead," where the octet is Italian ABBACDDC, all the octets are Shakespearian ABABCDCD. The sestets have sense, grammar and rhymes clumped as in the

Italian system. Brooke was more careful with his rhymes than usual. Except for one "o'er," he avoided the jarring antique words and shifted beats with which he had wilfully sprinkled so many earlier poems. Prosody, vocabulary, and imagery join in the traditionalistic stateliness which Milton, for example, would have sought as the prime effect;

The argument of these sonnets as "philosophy" is vaguely harmonious. Taken together, they speak for death over life. Their free-floating main source was to be found in Platonic philosophy, Christian dogmatics, and previous versifications of the patriotic impulse; and specific lines and phrases were drawn from Donne, Browning, Thomas Hardy, and Hilaire Belloc, and from notes made by Brooke himself years earlier, for other uses. Their reasoning simply collapses when refered to any intellectual test, even the test of consistency. Thus the life which is sacrificially abandoned is displayed as beautiful and happy in three poems, "The Dead" going so far as to praise even that old horror of Brooke's, the "unhoped serene / That men call age." By this means the principle of sacrifice is emphasized; the dead have abandoned great treasures. In "The Treasure," however, all the experience of this life is unwrapped again in the next, so that nothing is lost. In "Safety" the paradoxical idea that death protects man from all evils, not excepting "death's endeavor," similarly cancels out sacrifice. In "Peace," the most belligerent of these poems, the world left behind is shown as terrible, and the dead who leave it as lucky to get away —

> as swimmers leaping
> Glad from a world grown old and cold and weary,
> Leave the sick hearts that honour could not move,
> And half-men, and their dirty songs and dreary,
> And all the little emptiness of love.

So in these later three sonnets the death of a soldier becomes an advantage. The concept of sacrifice is therefore muddled even as regards the world supposed to be left behind.

A similar muddledness characterizes the future into which the dead procede. "The Dead (II)" handles this important matter with beautiful and precise imagery. The dead in that sonnet drop away from color, motion, and warmth, and in a manner turn solid:

> There are waters blown by changing winds to laughter
> And lit by the rich skies, all day. And after,

> Frost, with a gesture, stays the waves that dance
> And wandering loveliness. He leaves a white
> Unbroken glory, a gathered radiance,
> A width, a shining peace, under the night.

In "The Treasure" and "The Soldier" death hardly occurs, since the new existence retains the best of the old, or possibly all of it. The speaker in the first of these dies into "some golden space," losing color, light, dancing girls, and birdsong in the old existence, only to find it in the new:

> [There] I'll unpack that scented store
> Of song and flower and sky and face,
> And count, and touch, and turn them o'er.

In "The Soldier," most famous of all these sonnets, everybody wins. "The corner of a foreign field / That is forever England" is improved because of the "richer dust" buried there. But the original existence, called "heart," is not lost. It still beats, with "all evil shed away," as "pulse in the eternal mind." In "The Dead (I)" the new world of the dead becomes abstractions: Holiness, Honor, Love, Nobleness, and oddly, Pain. In "Safety" it becomes just safety, a term used four times in company with four synonyms meaning the same. Only in "Peace," where the world of the living is so ugly and evil, does the idea of extinction really suffice as the idea of death. "Peace" contains some verbal bargains, especially in the sestet, and its conclusion — "the worst friend and enemy is but death" — holds all that is worst in sentimental mysticism. However, this poem is alone in presenting a harmonious and self-consistent general plan of here and hereafter.

Seeing the poems in proof, Brooke commented "God, they're in the rough, these five camp-children of mine."[9] In his view "The Dead (II)" and "The Soldier" were best, a view probably based on the beautiful sestet of "The Dead (II)" and that celebrated octet of "The Soldier" which has stirred the emotions of people all over the world. In these sonnets about England he had managed to avoid mentioning cities, railroads, economic affairs, and the dole, filling out the gaps with the landscape data and friendship data of his old resource. His letters as he

---

9. Hassall, *Brooke*, p. 481.

approached extinction had become filled with wistful references to marriage and children. Passing over the women he loved more and the women he liked more, he asked Katherine Cox to look after one or two business matters he would have to leave unfinished. "I'm telling the Ranee that after she's dead, you're to have my papers. They may want to write a biography! How am I to know if I shan't be eminent? " He had commenced this letter, "I suppose you're about the best I can do in the way of a widow."[10] "The Dead (I)" – "Blow out, you bugles" – has a newer preoccupation in its regret not only for soldiers killed but for "those who would have been / Their sons ... their immortality."

V

The question of what Brooke might have accomplished if he had lived a few more decades had almost been answered by the time of his death. I judge that his slight talent had not only peaked, but moved along in its downward curve. His career, and in some senses his life, demonstrate a sort of compression or telescoping, a speeding up of time, as it were, which permitted his getting past seventy years in twenty-seven. All the regular movements of a writer's life are to be seen in him. Empty technique, formal cynicism, *Sturm und Drang,* crash and despair, then a reconciliation followed by an elder-statesman period in which advice and exhortation become important – Brooke would not have liked to think so, but he had recapitulated the long-lived poets of other ages. Among the officially national poets he is microscopic but complete: a pocket Wordsworth, a sketch of Tennyson, a crisp syllabus, perhaps, for the works of T. S. Eliot.

His work after the sonnets of 1914 suggest his knowing that he was past it all. He knew enough about that war to understand that the odds were against his surviving the one campaign, let alone the war; and his wistfulness about "being blown through pain to nothingness" may have affected his poetry. In any case he completed nothing except a song-lyric written to order for Denis Browne, who commanded a platoon alongside his but was continuing with music. The starts he made were coherent final

10. Brooke, *Letters,* p. 669.

parts of the curve of his career. Noting, as a responsible officer does, that his men were human, he tried a patriotic poem in working-class language:

> "When Nobby tried," the stokers say,
> "To stop a shrapnel with his belly,
> He [left blank] away,
> He left a lump of bleeding jelly."

> But he went out, did Nobby Clark,
> Upon the illimitable dark,
> Out of the fields where soldiers stray,
> Beyond parade, beyond reveille.

Unfinished and just as well. He aimed at a sonnet in which a song heard from the troops' quarters on the *Grantully Castle* turned out to be the same song "you" sang on a hillside in April, when "the woods were gold; and youth was in our hands." He imagined a widow and generalized from her to a world of ruined things: "Oh lovers parted, / Oh all you lonely over all the world." He was headed for Homer's country, and naturally tried poems invoking sons of Troy and Greece – Achilles, Sarpedon, Hector, "Priam and his fifty sons." But in his main efforts he was death-bound and personal. These include an Elegy on himself, a Threnody on England which advanced along the same lines as the sonnets, but with several voices, and a strange, ghostly, thin-voiced, genuinely moving, lyrical monologue in which he presented himself as actually dead.

In the Elegy he meant to speak of himself in the third person as "gone back to earth / Easily mingling," and yet surviving in some way, obscurely, known to "a few minds." The victim is now clothed in "quiet," "stillness," and "silence," terms which are given in sonorous though inaccurate images. The reciprocal Platonism of the sonnets would apparently have been the thesis of his Threnody on England. There the nation would be presented as thought:

> All things are written on the mind.
> There the sure hills have station; and the wind
> blows [blank space] in that placeless air.

Mind-England is shown to have birds, stars, light, "the waters that we love," and – crowding one another – both woods and trees.

This England of Edwardian poetry is both created in the mind and creative of the mind, in a strange mutual genesis. The stychomythic voices which elaborate the crux seem to predict choruses of T. S. Eliot, saying –

> She is not here, or now——
> She is here, and now, yet nowhere——
> We gave her birth, who bore us——

Some sort of ethical tension was also designed for the poem. A bad collection of persons, including "traitors," fail to participate in the task of creating England or being created by her:

> . . . This man, giving all for gold
> . . . That who has found evil good . . . . Those
> blind millions, bought and sold.

Some drawing back is visible here, and probably records misgivings about the "we" which had gone unchallenged in the sonnets, but which was terribly open to challenge by that sprawling majority of Britons whose ideas about life and death would be unrepresented in the Threnody. In a letter to Marsh, Brooke synopsised this poem as "the existence – and non-locality – of England," and added, "it contains the line – *'In Avons of the heart her rivers run.'* Lovely, isn't it?" "Lovely" is surely an irony. Avon, Heart, and England are a hard combination to put down; but the Avon is after all a river, and the image of a river running in a river is too fallacious for Brooke to have praised even in his own work. Marsh took the judgment seriously, and, followed by later biographers, printed it as an example of patriotic eloquence.

Weary and sick, tired of eloquence, not really wanting to die, Brooke cut off each of these efforts after the first thrust. In a single instance he pushed on farther, structurally completing the poem, though never getting to the finishing touches. It came into print under the name of "Fragment":

> I strayed about the deck, an hour, tonight
> Under a cloudy moonless sky; and peeped
> In at the windows, watched my friends at table,
> Or playing cards, or standing in the doorway,
> Or coming out into the darkness. Still
> No one could see me.
>
>   I would have thought of them
> – Heedless, within a week of battle – in pity,

Pride in their strength and in the weight and firmness
And link'd beauty of bodies, and pity that
This gay machine of splendour 'ld soon be broken,
Thought little of, pashed, scattered . . . .

Only, always,
I could but see them — against the lamplight — pass
Like coloured shadows, thinner than filmy glass,
Slight bubbles, fainter than the wave's faint light,
That broke to phosphorus out in the night,
Perishing things and strange ghosts — soon to die
To other ghosts — this one, or that, or I.

In this poem more than any other, Brooke combined all the best possibilities — egotism, the friendship idea, youth, outdoor-indoor contrast, coarse images jostling against lovely ones, varied verse, a touch of idea, and, in macabre prophesy, the absolute isolation of his doomed self as first to go — all from the happily conceived position of a spirit looking into a bright wardroom at friends playing cards. If he is scheduled to die, and then actually dead, in the other poems of 1914 and 1915, here he is looking back as from a great distance. And his short, self-observant, generally unhappy life is perfectly rounded.

Chapter Ten

"HOW TO KNOW IF I SHAN'T BE EMINENT"

When war was declared on August 2, 1914, Brooke made the mental and emotional commitments which are recorded in "An Unusual Young Man," but failed to commit himself to any practical action. His idea of military service was still romantic, and began and ended in images of himself and other loyal Britons repulsing German landing-parties on the beaches of Cornwall or Kent. The rural population of France was being called into service, and he thought for some days of going to France as a farm worker, "helping to get the crops in." The war-correspondent idea recurred, and he confided it to Violet Asquith; but the Prime Minister's daughter was caustic about the "egotism" in that idea of service, and he abandoned it with apologies. After some thought of serving as an enlisted man in respect to the levelling ideas of Socialism, he began to drill with a unit of London militia "made up of lawyers," and sent in his name as an applicant for officer training. Dropping out of that, he applied for a commission in the Territorials through the Cambridge headquarters. The commission which reached him first was that of sub-lieutenant or ensign in the Naval Reserve, with assignment to the Royal Naval Division. The RND had passed in and out of British history on various other occasions, and had been, by happy coincidence, John Donne's division in the wars against Spain. In 1914 it was being reorganized as a marine unit directly under the eye of Winston Churchill. Brooke and his fellow-officers soon came to think of it as an elite force, with special talents and a special destiny.

As shown in a previous chapter, Brooke soon learned the rhythms of life in a rifle unit. Some terse notes he made in a notebook during the Antwerp campaign show his ability to catch essentials: entrenching-tools, gun-bursts, burning oil-tanks, the dull streams of hopeless refugees, observation aircraft, directions of bombardments, notes on a lost soldier, "Harrington," and little sketches of the trench positions.[1] After the retreat to England, he

1. Brooke Papers, King's College.

developed the skills of a platoon leader. Brought into contact with Britons of the working classes for the first time in his life, he was at first amused and supercilious. For several months he made routine jokes about their habits and forms of speech, and about their poverty and ignorance. Towards Christmas of 1914, a change in his feelings is reflected in his letters. Little passages about the separate personalities and individual problems of the private soldiers begin to appear. By February or March, he had developed a feeling of identification with the platoon as a whole, and had reached a position of friendly understanding with its individual members. His health was rapidly breaking down, and he spent weekends and sometimes weeks resting in the homes of the great families of his new acquaintance, but meanwhile continued to develop his common touch. In 1915, standing under arms, ready for a landing below the cliffs of a Turkish seacoast, he reached a pleasing unity with his platoon.

> Slowly the day became wan and green and the sea opal. Everyone's face looked drawn and ghastly. If we landed, my company would be the first to land—— We made out that we were only a mile or two from a dim shore. I was seized with an agony of remorse that I hadn't taught my platoon a thousand things more energetically and competently. The light grew. The shore looked to be crammed with Fate, and most ominously silent. One man thought he saw a camel through his glasses——
>
> There were some hours of silence.
>
> About seven someone said "we're going home." [that is, back into the Agean Sea] We dismissed the stokers [soldiers], who said, quietly, "when's the next battle? "; and disempanoplied, and had another breakfast.[2]

The identification was almost complete, even to the little soldierly joke against high command which he not only relished but participated in.

Had the landing taken place at that time, killing Brooke along with his platoon and tens of thousands of other people, his reputation would have taken a different course. The destiny of the Royal Naval Division had been a long time getting known. After the Antwerp expedition the Division had settled down to retrain as an attack unit. The training area was in Dorset, and Brooke

2. Brooke, *Letters*, pp. 674-75.

found it romantic to manoeuver, even in mud, on the scenes of old battles of Druid and Roman, Celt and Saxon. It was then thought that the Division would go to France. By the late fall of 1915, the murderous nature of the trench warfare on the Western Front was well enough known. There, the chief industrial powers of the world had abandoned tactics and settled down to an exchange of young lives and high explosives along a single line of trenches that hardly moved at all. Brooke understood this kind of warfare, and expected to die in it. "Well, we're doing our best," he wrote to a friend in Berkeley. "But it's a bloody thing, half the youth of Europe being blown through pain to nothingness, in the incessant mechanical slaughter of these modern battles. I can only wonder at human endurance."[3] By November, 1914, when he wrote the letter, most of his contemporaries at Cambridge were already feeding off into the butchery of the Western Front. Many of his poet friends were to die there. His brother Alfred went there and was dead within a few weeks. Ultimately the Royal Naval Division would go there. On the Western Front it was destined to become, like other divisions, a sort of conduit pipe into which tens of thousands of men were fed, draft by draft, into the murderous fire. Lost as outright battle-deaths. the smallish RND counted some 592 officers and 10,925 other ranks. Among the fourteen original officers in Brooke's Hood Battalion, most died at Gallipoli a week or two after his death, and all but two, Bernard Freyberg and Arthur Asquith, were dead by the end of the war.

Freyberg's last appearance in the Brooke literature is gallant enough. Denis Browne, before dying, noticed him swimming between ships assembled for the landing under bombardment from the Turkish batteries. The act suited the campaign. The Dardanelles effort had Churchill for its principal sponsor, and was full of the Churchill flair. Its aim was to invade Turkey at the point where Asia thrusts westward into the longitudes of Europe, to open the Bosphorus to Allied shipping, and to capture Constantinople. A victory of this kind could take Turkey out of the war, and the disappearance of Turkey would secure British interests in the Eastern Mediterranean, and at the same time release the Balkan armies of Russia for service against Germany, with the completion of circular effect occuring in relaxation of

3. Brooke, *Letters,* p. 633.

pressure on the fixed Western Front. Its effects would therefore spread over Africa, Asia, and Europe, and its success would be of the most universal benefit to England and her allies. On the other hand, professional soldiers doubted whether it could succeed, and only the fierce politics of Churchill could get it mounted at all. Later, after it had bloodily and expensively failed, Churchill was forced out of his office as First Sea Lord, and made to wait another quarter-century for greatness in the rôle of war leader.

Brooke's early fame was closely bound to the campaign and its failure. In March, 1915, he led his platoon on board the *Grantully Castle,* a liner converted to a troopship, and began his final flood of letters home. These grew more and more serious as the ship entered the Mediterranean, stopped at Malta, and proceeded eastward. By the first week of April he was making his plans for death in a series of letters on the disposal of his effects. His ship was in the Agean sea, then Alexandria, where he fell ill of sunstroke and camp diarrhea. Refusing a staff appointment, he crept back onto the ship, threatened Turkey again without landing, and was carried into a series of anchorages in the Greek islands. Still sick, he wrote his little "Fragment," the whisper of a dead man. The final anchorage, for him, was in Trebuki Bay, under the looming peak of Mount Pephko near the southern end of the island Skyros. His insect bites were opening as strep infections. He went ashore for attack exercises with his platoon, but returned exhausted, and went to his bunk early. Next day, April 20, he learned that one of his war sonnets, "The Soldier," had been read in Westminster Abbey by Dean Inge, the best-known Anglican priest of that day, and had been compared to its disadvantage against a passage in the Book of Isaiah. Brooke said, as a final comment on his career, that "he was sorry Inge did not think him quite as good as Isaiah." His friends recognised all at once that he might die, and began to make notes in their diaries.[4] General Paris took part. General Sir Ian Hamilton, commander of the whole expedition, moved to prevent or assist. Some fifteen doctors, British and then French, gave opinions. The radios sent their messages. Churchill was notified, then Marsh, then Mrs. Brooke. More diary entries.

4. Various breathless accounts of his death, including those of Browne, Asquith, Quilter, and Hamilton, are reprinted in Hassall, *Brooke,* and Brooke, *Letters.*

The fleet was due to sail for its more general slaughter, but kept its attention fixed on Brooke. Anticipating his death, Churchill asked a relative to attend the funeral, if possible, as his personal representative, adding sonorously, "we shall not see his like again." Naval radio brought Mrs. Brooke's last message to her son's bedside. General Hamilton radioed again to Marsh and Churchill. "The first-born of the intellect must die," he jotted in his diary. "Is *That* the answer to the riddle? " In London, newspaper briefed themselves. April 23 – St. George's Day. The fleet seemed to stand still in the blue water, waiting.

II

Brooke's genius for appearing in the best light had never operated as well as this. With his actual death a dozen of the tangled threads of romance and history seemed to come together. The burial, in a green valley overlooking the port, was handled with all the ritual Brooke's friends could wring out of the traditions of religion, warfare, and romantic history. It was the holy day of St. George, the patron saint of England, and also the anniversary of Shakespeare's birth and death. It was a crusader ocean; he could be a new Christian hero, delivering Constantinople from the Moslems. An epitaph in Greek, scribbled by a translator on the crosspiece of his wooden grave-marker, called him "The Soldier of God." Much more, he died in Homer's country, in Ulysses's ocean, at the very island where Achilles had lived. Helen had passed that way. East and West had first divided on these shores; and he had speculated about the possibility of killing his Turk, as Achilles had killed his three thousand years before, on the very plains of Troy.

Now the promotion began. Brooke had died alone, individually, not in the anonymous muddle of a mass slaughter. The emotions of the British people, now writhing in expressionless agony over the latter kind of death, were ready for a sudden leap towards Brooke's own unique kind. His sonnets permitted it to be said that he had laid down his life joyfully and beautifully. Marsh immediately pointed this out in *The Times,* arguing that often "seeming waste is not waste," and that no waste had truly occured in "a young life full of promise and willingly laid down." This preamble was followed by the great diapaison of Churchill's testimonial, also in *The Times*:

Rupert Brooke is dead. A telegram from the Admiralty at Lemnos tells us that this life has closed at the moment when it seemed to have reached its springtime. A voice had become audible, a note had been struck, more true, more thrilling, more able to do justice to the nobility of our youth in arms engaged in this present war, than any other – more able to express their thoughts of self-surrender, and with a power to carry comfort to those who watched them so intently from afar. The voice has been swiftly stilled. Only the echoes and the memory remain; but they will linger.

During the last few months of his life, months of preparation in gallant comradeship and open air, the poet-soldier told with all the simple force of genius the sorrow of youth about to die, and the sure triumphant consolations of a sincere and valiant spirit. He expected to die; he was willing to die for the dear England whose beauty and majesty he knew; and he advanced towards the brink in perfect serenity, with absolute conviction of the rightness of his country's cause, and a heart devoid of hate for fellow-men.

The thoughts to which he gave expression in the very few incomparable war sonnets which he has left behind will be shared by many thousands of young men moving resolutely and blithely forward into this, the hardest, the cruellest, and the least-rewarded of all the wars that men have fought. They are a whole history and revelation of Rupert Brooke himself. Joyous, fearless, versatile, deeply instructed, with classic symmetry of mind and body, he was all that one would wish England's noblest sons to be in days when no sacrifice but the most precious is acceptable, and the most precious is that which is most freely proffered.[5]

These bell-tones assured the establishment of Brooke's life and death as a business of national importance. They presented Brooke as England's hero, but as a hero of such brilliance and force as to transcend nations and serve as a cultural hero, a figure of myth.

In a sophisticated society, myth and symbol may be identified even as they develop. Henry James quickly placed Brooke in cultural psychology, saying that his death gave "a pride and a refinement of beauty and poetry" to "those splendid sonnets – which will enrich our whole collective consciousness." Gilbert Murray, at Cambridge, noticed that his dead student would "probably live in fame as an almost mythical figure." From his different viewpoint of despair and horror, D. H. Lawrence wrote

5. *The Times* (London), April 26, 1916.

to Lady Ottoline Morrell, "Bright phoebus smote him down. It is all in the saga. O God. O God, it is all too much of a piece; it is like madness." Even those who had mocked at Brooke suddenly came around. "In spite of all we have said," noted Maynard Keynes in Bloomsbury, "I find myself crying for him." Meanwhile the public press was active. Brooke was naturally compared to the soldier-patriot Philip Sidney, to the martyr-poet Byron, and to other willing sacrifices like Christ and Socrates. "To look at, he was part of the youth of the world," wrote an editor of *The Daily News.* *The Star* called him "the youth of our race in symbol." Hassall, whose chapter "Man into Marble" gives best account of these posthumous transactions, adds that "memorial verses of good intent but gruelly sentimentality proliferated in the press.... Elegies appeared on all sides, and even a morsel beginning *If You should die, think only this of me,* somehow found its way into print."[6] *New Numbers,* in which the sonnets were printed, was immediately sold out, but the sonnets were quickly reprinted in other journals and were read in schools, preached about, and wept over.

As this movement went on, the Gallipoli campaign began and faltered, began again, lost force, and settled down to the simple exchange of explosives and young men which was familiar on the Western Front. Government shifted, Sir Ian Hamilton was removed from command, Churchill went to France as commander of an infantry battalion, Marsh got ready the next number of *Georgian Poets,* this time featuring Brooke's sonnets. The myth and legend continued to be sweeter to contemplate than any reality then available.

III

With a perversity that can only be laid to jealousies, first toward the nation, then toward one another, Brooke's old friends pranced among the opportunities of concealment, revelation, manipulation, and reconstruction. Even before the withdrawal of the shattered Gallipoli force, these people had begun to protest that the Brooke of the hero-myth was not the Brooke that they

6. For locations of these and other reactions, see Hassall, *Brooke,* pp.514ff.

had known, not – as they put it – the real Rupert Brooke. The general impulse made for establishment of the "Young Apollo, laughing-eyed," of Francis Cornford's early epigram.

The trouble naturally began in Rugby and Cambridge. In the *Cambridge Review* for May, 1915, John Shepherd asserted clumsily, "While it is not easy, we owe it to him not to comfort ourselves by letting our thoughts dwell on a mythical being who was not Rupert, and whose loss is therefore the easier to bear." Friendly editors in such journals as *The New Statesman* and the *Cambridge Magazine* agreed that the national legend had "grown around an imaginary figure very different from the real man." An important contribution came from Henry James, who proposed in his Introduction to *Letters From America* that Brooke was untransferable into print, existing only in "the simple act of presence and communication." Presence and communication are, of course, the properties of Christ and Holy Mass; and lest the reader miss this connection, James also said that "Rupert expressed us *all,* at the highest tide of our actuality." Walter de la Mare, who had become an heir to Brooke's estate and copyrights, had preserved an idea of Brooke's giving "the happy shining impression that he must have come . . . from another planet." Stunned by the memory, de la Mare gulped in print, not originally, that "Brooke was himself the happiest, most complex, and characteristic of his poems." Synonyms for "golden" and "sun-god" piled up for years. De la Mare topped "golden" with "radium." Brooke's theatrical friend Maurice Browne, feeling himself shoved aside by the Cambridge group, tortured semantics so far as to declare, in print, that Brooke and the golden myths were inseparable because "the man *was* the myth." Holbrook Jackson, a good critic sometimes, was blinded by the brightness, judged that what Brooke really stood for was "the Joy of Life," and concluded preposterously, "there is really nothing to tell about his life but his enjoyment of it."

There was lots to tell. There was too much. It had fallen to Edward Marsh to write the official biography and create the official edition of the letters. Marsh approached his task full of knowledge, but also full of scruple. He managed to suppress every mean, silly, and unfortunate passage in Brooke's life, and to present the national myth and the Apollo myth as it were together. His tone was that of Winston Churchill's tribute, which he quoted in his final paragraphs as almost the last word. The only word he found fit to follow Churchill's was that of Denis Browne, who had sailed past "Rupert's Island" two days before his own death. Browne had described a beautiful sunset. The island, that of Achilles, Rupert, Jaqueline Onassis, or whomever, had a "crimson golden halo" lying around it. "Every colour had come into the sea and sky to do him honour; and it seemed that the island must ever be shining with his glory that we buried there."[7] That ought to have done it. But even as Marsh Christized his beloved friend, criticisms were coming in. Jealous of Marsh, Mary Ruth Brooke insisted that his biography was not "complete." Her "corrections" to Marsh's manuscripts show a kind of genius in finding indiscretions Marsh had missed. Brooke had said in a letter that her widowhood home in Rugby had a number, though "I've always lived in a house with a name before." That could not be printed. Brooke in early August, 1914, "didn't quite immediately realize that he must fight." That, with a collection of other items just as innocent, had to go. In a world in which Sybil Pye was writing that "Rupert's movements" as a chorus chanter in a Cambridge play were "like those of Nijinsky . . . when in the following Autumn he [Nijinsky] danced the *Rose* for the first time," Marsh's golden youth, again gold-plated by Mrs. Brooke, could and did stand.[8]

There were other views. Ezra Pound had respected Brooke as a man and as a poet, and now wrote scathingly to Harriet Monroe, in Chicago, about the impossible excellence of the Apollo image. Walter de la Mare and his two fellow-heirs, Wilfrid Gibson and Lascelles Abercrombie, spoke about it with amusement even as they promoted it in poems, lectures and articles. Surely in irony, a reviewer in the *Oxford Magazine* judged that Brooke "seems to have missed the uplifting education that the passion of love would have afforded him." Those who had known him kept insisting that their special knowledge meant a special relationship. In the middle 1920's, unveiling a monument to the RND, a speaker said that "Brooke's verses" are "printed in newspapers, written in books, blotted by tears, carved upon stone. But they belong to us, the

7. Marsh's Memoir in Brooke, *Collected Poems* (1918), p. clvi.
8. Marsh's manuscript with Mrs. Brooke's annotations is in the Brooke Papers, King's College.

Royal Naval Division." Brooke was claimed, then unclaimed, for Rugby. When his memorial plaque was unveiled in the Chapel, Margaret Keynes wrote that the solemn activities "had absolutely no relation to Rupert at all." Her Brooke was different from Rugby's Brooke. This was the par. The superhuman excellence of Brooke as begun by Churchill and completed by Marsh was let to stand before the public. But each person who had known him claimed to have known him better. Where the mob found a sacrificed hero, each found a personal god. The rest of the story of Brooke biography, as opposed to Brooke criticism, is made up of attempts to break through the frozen perfections of their young Apollo.

IV

Like his identities as a sacrificial hero and a golden Apollo, Brooke's identity as a poet was laid down in iron lines by Churchill. Churchill's interest was lodged in the war sonnets. He judged these to be masterpieces of their kind, lumping them with the military and patriotic poems of Kipling, Henley, and Housman. It was with honest feeling for his nation and its young men that he proclaimed Brooke the spokesman for people of military age, the "many thousands of young men moving resolutely and blithely forward" into the war. Over the decades, criticism and judgment have moved in other directions. Speculatively, they have ranged among questions of potential, technical merit, reception, permanence. They have characteristically been weakened by dependence upon the touchstone and talismanic system, or anti-system, and by the various jealousies of class, clique, and social circle. Perhaps the single lapse they have not fallen into is that of extreme over-evaluation. Brooke was never rated better than a minor poet. The dramatic question was whether he could stay in the ratings at all.

The speculative question of potential had gathered some negative responses even before Brooke died. Stilled for a while in the years of his mythic triumphs, it was raised again after 1919. It asked whether Brooke's death had really cut off a developing career. Bloomsbury thought not. Forster saw Brooke as a politician or bureau executive, callings suitable to his "mixture of toughness and idealism." Virginia Woolf took the same lines. She "didn't think much of his poetry." In a careful but absolute judgment, written in 1925, she called his war poems "barrel-organ music" and remembered his other poems as "all adjectives and contortions." Her speculation was that Brooke was destined "to be a member of Parliament and edit the classics, a very powerful ambitious man, but not a poet."[9] Ben Keeling and Lord Dalton had thought of his becoming, like them, a successful Socialist politician. Maurice Browne's touch with him had been through the stage, and Browne cited his fascination with drama as showing that "had Brooke lived, his main work would have been dramatic."[10]

Even among literary people there was hardly a consensus. Wilfried Gibson refused to certify what the world had lost through Brooke's death. In his Howland address at Harvard, an undertaking in which he stood as it were in Brooke's own shoes, de la Mare substituted a cheap personalism for educated speculation. "What, if he had lived, he would have done in this world is a fascinating but unanswerable question. This only can be said, that he would have gone on being his wonderful self. Radium is inexhaustible." After his lifetime of consideration, Sir Geoffrey Keynes remained uncertain. Brooke's gift, he wrote in 1967, "was . . . silenced prematurely" and "deprived of the opportunity to unfold its true worth." But Keynes had never been sure:

> When Brooke died it was not primarily the poet his friends mourned. It was rather the sense that an outstanding personality and intellect had been extinguished. His poetic faculties might have increased in power, or perhaps they would have waned with the growth of more critical and scholarly perceptions. His creativeness might have taken quite other turns, but we believed he would have left his mark in some unexpected way on the life of England.[11]

Scholars who move through the masses of manuscript scribbling which Brooke left behind are likely to agree that many possibilities still lay open for him. His steady ambition and ability to manipulate people show that something would have happened; and that he had not achieved acceptance in circles of the

---

9. Quoted in Hassall, *Brooke*, p. 529.
10. *Recollections of Brooke*, p. 52.
11. Introduction to Brooke, *Letters*, p. xiii.

University, the press, the aristocracy, and the government, only to turn mute and inglorious afterwards.

The question of what he had actually made in his capacity as poet or maker ought to have been easier to answer, but was not. After 1919 Brooke's poetry faced a criticism which was harsh, demanding, and unfriendly in its nature, and which was particularly suspicious of exactly the qualities for which his poetry was best known. F. R. Leavis's tone of contempt and technique of impossible comparisons are typical:

> Brooke had a considerable personal force and became himself an influence. He energized the Garden-Suburb ethos with a certain original talent and the vigour of a prolonged adolescence. His verse exhibits a genuine sensuousness rather like Keat's (though more energetic) and something that is rather like Keat's vulgarity with a Public School accent.

To Babette Deutsch, a few years later, Brooke seemed a futile poetaster who "liked to drink a tea in an old garden." Such judgments have the shining beauty of the pin by which a butterfly is pinned to a card. Against them, and against similar arraignments, stood the inescapable fact that Brooke's poetry was delightful to readers. De la Mare called attention to the pleasures Brooke registered through discovery of "the sudden flowering miracle of the ordinary." "Frankness," "ingenuity," and "humor," were the qualities Monro found in him. Ezra Pound was concerned to separate him from his contemporaries, and wrote:

> He was the best of the younger English, though Eliot is certainly more interesting.
>
> Brooke flocked with the stupidest set of blockheads to be found in any country, i.e. the Abercrombie, Drinkwater, New Numbers assortment and that certainly did not promise much for him, still he was infinitely better than his friends.[12]

Brooke would have understood F. R. Leavis and Babette Deutsch even less than they understood him. All technical criticism droops before the fact that his verse was lyrical, charming, and companionable. Edward Thomas was enough older to lay these merits to "aspiration" and "the unfulfilled eagerness of ambitious self-conscious youth." Any fair reader will notice his

12. 21 September, 1915, quoted in Noel Stock, *The Life of Ezra Pound* (London, 1970), p. 182.

desire to charm, or, as Hassall puts it, "the magnanimous view, an evident zeal to win over, communicate, and share." Compton Mackenzie, who had begun his career in the relaxed manner in which Brooke had begun his, and who had also looked at the barbed-wire beaches of Turkey in 1915, liked to contrast Brooke with the "shoddy realists" who traduced his poetical character in the 1930's and 1940's. "To pretend that Brooke is not a figure on which the imaginative mind may dwell with greater exhaltation than on some pale trembling junket of a creature whose melting-point becomes the center of interest in a book or play," Mackenzie wrote in 1967, "is mere wantonness."[13] Charm best matches charm in an opinion given to Edward Garnett by Lawrence of Arabia. Off his camel, out of his desert princedom, down from his colonelcy, serving at a desolate Indian station as private in the RAF, the author of *Seven Pillars of Wisdom* called attention to some poems he liked — "The Fish" and some sonnets. "Don't you like Rupert Brooke's sonnets? " he asked. "They are wonderful, especially for a man who was not very good at anything he wrote— God almighty! Must everyone be as sevenleagued as Milton and Byron and Hardy? "[14]

The question of Brooke's ability to survive among the standard poets is still raised among technical critics. Besides its slightness in mass and idea, the work suffers by the prominence within it of unacceptable positions and dubious workmanship. The war poems please fewer readers than they offend, and the young Apollo presented by surviving friends has its repellent as well as its attractive side. Charm has been thought not to be enough. Anthologists have been doubtful. The final myth about Brooke was, however, the myth of his extinction. People still like to read Brooke. His readership has changed somewhat in character, but hardly flagged in number. Even as he was being chased out of the game by formal criticism, he was establishing himself as part of the total literary heritage. By 1954, some 600 000 copies of the various editions had been sold. Perhaps the sale is now over a million. Marsh's edition, *The Collected Poems,* continued to sell even after Keynes's edition, *The Poetical Works,* came on the market. One or other of these books has gone into a new edition

13. *My Life and Times,* Octave 6 (London, 1967), p. 131.
14. *Letters of T. E. Lawrence,* ed. David Garnett (London, 1938), p. 612.

or new impression almost every year since the first appeared in 1918. Other books have bobbed out in their wake: the *John Webster*, the *Letters from America*, Keynes' *Bibliography*, the *Letters* edited by Keynes, the miscellanies edited by Hassall and by Rogers, the generous and beautiful biography by Hassall, the furious anti-biography of Michael Hastings, and the reminiscences – so many of them – by old friends passing from the scene. Of the hundred poets who were publishing in the London of Brooke's generation only Yeats, Eliot, and Pound are so well known and widely read. Brooke's eminence is not at all like theirs, but it is an eminence.

SELECTED BIBLIOGRAPHY

Primary Sources

Poems by Rupert Brooke. London: Sidgwick and Jackson, 1911.
1914 and Other Poems. London: Sidgwick and Jackson, 1915.
Lithuania. Chicago: Chicago Little Theater, 1915.
John Webster and the Elizabethan Drama. New York: John Lane, 1916.
Letters from America. With an Introduction by Henry James. London: Sidgwick and Jackson, and New York, Scribners, 1916.
The Collected Poems of Rupert Brooke. With a Memoir by Edward Marsh. London: Sidgwick and Jackson, 1918.
The Poetical Works of Rupert Brooke. Edited by Geoffrey Keynes. London: Faber and Faber, 1946.
Democracy and the Arts. London: Rupert Hart-Davis, 1946.
The Prose of Rupert Brooke. Edited by Christopher Hassall. London: Sidgwick and Jackson, 1956.
The Letters of Rupert Brooke. Edited by Geoffrey Keynes. London: Faber and Faber, 1968.
Rupert Brooke: a Reappraisal and Selection. Edited by Timothy Rogers, with comment by the same. London: Routledge and Kegan Paul, 1971.
(Less important publications, serial publications, and later editions of the above publications, are described in Keynes's *Bibliography,* below.)

Secondary Sources

Bibliographies

Keynes, Geoffrey. *A Bibliography of the Works of Rupert Brooke.* London: Rupert Hart-Davis, 1954. Third edition, revised, 1964. Gives all known printed writings, plus manuscript writings.
Rogers, Timothy. Appended to his *Rupert Brooke,* 1971. Excellent list of books and articles about Brooke.

Books

Browne, Maurice. *Recollections of Rupert Brooke.* Chicago: The Author,

1927. Republished Port Washington, N.Y.; Kennikat Press, 1968. Browne knew Brooke in Chicago and London, and made a transatlantic crossing with him. Many letters are included.

Hassall, Christopher. *Rupert Brooke, A Biography*. London: Faber and Faber, 1964. A long, lyrical, beautifully detailed biography. The indispensable book.

Hastings, Michael. *The Handsomest Young Man in England*. London: Michael Joseph, 1967. Angry biography broken into separate debunking essays. Richly illustrated with old photographs.

Marsh, Edward. *Rupert Brooke: A Memoir*. Published with the *Collected Poems*, 1918 (above). By Brooke's faithful friend, who worked under the eye of Brooke's mother.

Rogers, Timothy. The "Reappraisal" sections of his *Rupert Brooke*, 1971 (above).

Ross, Robert H. *The Georgian Revolt*, 1910-1922. Carbondale: Southern Illinois University Press, 1967. Brooke as the central organizing figure of the movement.

Stringer, Arthur. *Red Wine of Youth*. With materials collected by Richard Haliburton. New York: Macmillan, 1948. Heavily sentimental, often inaccurate biography.

Urmitzer, Klara. *Rupert Brooke*. Würzburg, 1935. A Bonn doctoral dissertation, analytically designed.

Sections of Books

Asquith, Herbert. *Moments of Memory*. London, Hutchinson, 1937.

Foster, H. C. *At Antwerp and the Dardanelles*. London: Macmillan, 1918.

Garrod, H. W. *The Profession of Poetry*. London: Oxford University Press, 1929.

Grant, Joy. *Harold Monro and the Poetry Bookshop*. Berkeley: University of California Press, 1967.

Hassall, Christopher. *Edward Marsh: A Biography*. London: Faber and Faber, 1959.

Holroyd, Michael. *Lytton Strachey* (Vol. One). London: Heinemann, 1967.

Leavis, F. R. *New Bearings in English Poetry*. London: Chatto and Windus, 1932.

Marsh, Edward. *A Number of People*. London: Hamish Hamilton, 1939.

Wilson, Colin. *Poetry and Mysticism*. London: Hutchinson, 1970.

Woolf, Leonard. *Beginning Again*. London: Hogarth Press, 1964.

(A selection of periodical articles up to 1970 is offered in the Bibliography appended to Timothy Rogers, *Rupert Brooke*, 1971.)

Index

Q4